1001 Tips & Hints On Ceramics

by Dale Swant

TABLE OF CONTENTS

EIGHTH PRINTING

Published By:
SCOTT PUBLICATIONS
30595 EIGHT MILE
LIVONIA, MI 48152-1798
ISBN# 0-916809-81-1

No. 4249-3/96 PRINTED IN U.S.A.

Introduction

The great thing about doing ceramics is that we are always learning. Whether it be from a teacher, reading a magazine or from first hand experience, without this educational process your hobby might get a bit stale from time to time. Therefore, any new bits of information that you get a chance to pick up will be a bonus.

The purpose of this book is to give you one source of simple tips and hints that will help as you go along. Each section of the book includes specific information on each subject to make that particular product or tool a little easier to use. The general section will be of aid in that it tells you how to use everyday household items to make your ceramic efforts easier.

We think you will enjoy reading and working with this book and possibly pick up a few pointers along the way. It is by no means all the ideas floating around the ceramic industry but it is rather a compilation into one source of the more common ones. We've also left a page open at the end of the book for you to jot down any tips you pick up first hand.

This is the only book of its type that contains so much information in such little space and we hope that you enjoy and use it to make your ceramics easier and more fun.

Dale

Dale Swant

Stains

1. If you have a finish done in stains that you do not like you can remove it from your piece of bisque by refiring the piece. The stain will normally burn away although the piece may not be completely white. Just apply new stain coverage.

2. Stains are used only on bisque.

3. If you are having trouble removing translucent stains from your brushes, try using ordinary lemon oil furniture polish. Slightly dip brush and wipe out well. Oil will help condition brush. Since translucents are oil based, you only use this brush for oil base colors.

4. A special effect of woodgrain can be accomplished easily. Simply cover entire piece with your choice of translucent color and wipe piece down with a wrinkled piece of newspaper. Be sure to do your wiping in one direction. The newspaper will absorb some color leaving woodgrain streaks where the color remains.

5. Although not used too much today, buffing oil is great for evening or smoothing out stain finishes done in translucents. It will not remove all color and leaves a soft sheen.

6. To make application of non-firing metallics (brush-on or spray) even, apply a coat of opaque stain over the bisque and under your metallics. Since you are covering up the color used with a metallic you can use up bits of color you have in old jars, even several colors if you wish.

7. One of the basics to remember is that opaque stains may be mixed together and that translucent stains may be mixed together to attain a new color. You cannot however, mix translucent and opaque stains.

8. Before you antique a piece be sure to apply a good even coverage of either brush-on or spray fixative. This will prevent your translucent from being absorbed and also will help you remove it from unwanted areas more easily.

9. You are not limited to painting features with opaque stains. After spray fixing your opaque stains use the thick part from the lid or bottom of the jar of your translucent stains. Allow to dry and spray fix again.

10. Your antiquing will be much darker if you do not spray fix your opaque stains before antiquing. Your colors are much harder to control so be sure to practice a bit before attempting this.

11. Stains should only be used on pieces that are going to be used for decoration. Anything that comes in contact with heat or water should be finished in some variation of glaze.

12. Stains may be used on pieces that are going to be used outdoors. When finished, they should be sprayed with several coats of fixative to prevent moisture from penetrating. It is a good idea to have the inside glazed.

13. Although our primary interest is ceramics, stains may be used on a variety of items such as plaster, wood, cloth, etc.

14. If you are having trouble getting bisque pieces to absorb stains the way you think they should, try a vinegar and water solution rub down as the last step in cleaning. Don't over-do it as the vinegar will really eat into greenware if left unchecked.

15. If you cannot stain your bisque piece immediately after firing, store it in a plastic bag so that household dust and greases will not get on it and plug the pores.

16. An opaque stain is a color in the ceramic range of medias, which means it is solid in color and cannot be seen through.

17. Stains are murder on clothes so if you get some on you when painting, be sure to remove as soon as possible so that they will not set in the fabric.

18. Opaque stains are waterbase colors and should be thinned with water. All materials used in the application, etc., should be cleaned with water.

19. When you open a jar of stain be sure to clean the inside of the lid as soon as possible. If necessary let the lid soak to remove excess color. Once a dirty lid is replaced on a jar and the color dries, it is a real chore to remove again.

20. Correct application of opaque stains requires the use of a stiff brush. The bristles should be quite stiff so you can sort of scrub the color into the bisque.

21. You may find the going a bit easier when applying opaque stains to bisque if you slightly mist the piece with a spray bottle of water. Since your opaques are waterbase, the slight dampening will allow the color to flow on easier.

22. It is important to apply stains as smoothly as possible. Any blobs or overlap lines that are not brushed out during application will show on the finished piece.

23. Translucent stains, as the name implies, will allow the color underneath to be seen.

24. Most translucent stains used are oil base colors but some manufacturers do produce waterbase translucents so be sure to check the labels to find out which you have.

25. Mineral spirits is usually the cleaning or thinning agent used with oil base translucent stains.

26. Since translucent stains are used to accent your already applied opaques, you will apply them using a softer brush. You will usually apply color over a surface that has some protective coating to make the wiping back process easier.

27. Since the concentrated color pigment in translucent stains has a habit of settling to the bottom of the jar it is important to always mix colors thoroughly. This may necessitate shaking as well as stirring.

28. If you don't have the stain color you want, it is possible to create new colors by mixing like-base colors. Be sure to experiment with the colors you create on a piece of white paper, however, before applying to bisque.

29. If you would like to antique a piece finished in liquid bright gold, simply put your basic technique with translucent stains to work.

30. You can create a marble effect using your translucent stains. Simply pour a bit of several contrasting colors into a container of water large enough to emmerse your bisque piece. Stir the water with stain on top of it slightly and immediately dip your bisque piece into it. The color will adhere to the bisque leaving a marbled appearance. Be sure to hold piece in a non-vital area and do the dipping quickly. You can spray fix after it's dry.

31. If you do not like to use spray fixative it is possible to buff opaque stains to a satin-like sheen. Not all products will work this way so be sure to experiment a bit before attempting it on your favorite piece. A soft cloth like a diaper does a great job.

32. Usually one coat coverage of a piece with opaque stains is all that is necessary. You might find, however, that lighter colors require two. If you are trying to cover a darker color with a light shade, you may need several coats.

33. You may not know it but you can accomplish a variety of techniques in the lace draping field by using opaque stains mixed with white glue. Simply mix the two together, soak lace in the mixture and add to an already stained piece, such as a doll for decoration. The lace will dry hard and you will have the color you want.

34. Fixatives are usually used to seal stain work. Available in either a spray can or bottle for brush-on, they should be added to stained pieces to protect them from dust and grease and make them easier to clean with a damp rag. Fixatives keep your pieces from chipping as well.

35. Remember that pieces decorated with stains are not safe for food, nor are they dishwasher safe.

36. For an unusual decorating technique, you can spatter on colors by loading a brush with color, bending back the bristles and letting the paint fly. Also called flecking, the size of the drops you get is determined by how heavily you load your brush.

37. Opaque stains are ideal for use in brush techniques. The colors lend themselves to mixing and blending well.

38. Although most techniques call for antiquing with translucent stains, this same technique may be accomplished with opaques by thinning colors to half-water.

39. The best type of bisque for stains is that which has been fired to 06.

40. Dried stain will not liquify again.

41. Some recommend a scrubbing type action with your brush to begin the application of stains and then going back over with your brush to smooth color.

42. Metallic stains are usually used to decorate those areas that simulate metal but they can also be thinned and used in antiquing techniques.

43. Metallic stains can be mixed with other opaque stains for special decorating effects.

44. Metallic stains can be applied directly to bisque or over other opaque stains.

45. Metallic paste is a combination of metallic particles suspended in thick paste to help in the application.

46. Metallic pastes are generally used to accent detail and are generally an oil base product.

47. Metallic pastes are most commonly applied over another opaque color with a soft rag or finger tip.

48. Although often forgotten, it is best to seal paste metallics onto pieces with a coating of spray or brush-on fixative.

49. Normally the translucent stain color contrasts with the opaque colors already used on a piece.

50. Translucent stains are primarily used to accent the detail of a piece and may be either water or oil base.

51. Translucent stains can be used for a rouging technique when only a small bit of color is added to certain areas with a soft rag wrapped around your finger.

52. Translucent stains can be used directly on bisque rather than over sealed opaque stains, but they do soak in rapidly and are very hard to control.

53. Translucent stain colors are very difficult, if not impossible, to remove from clothing.

54. Most students get into the habit of antiquing pieces only with black or dark brown. These translucent stains are available in many colors and effective antiquing is possible using them. Example: A dark blue antiquing on a light blue piece.

55. When antiquing, only remove color from raised areas of a piece, leaving color in crevices to accent the detail.

56. If you remove too much color when wiping off translucent stains, you can re-apply and start the process all over again.

57. The amount of translucent stain you leave on a piece will determine the lightness or darkness of your entire finished piece.

58. The drying time for translucent stains is longer than that for opaque stains.

59. Since translucent stains are in the oil-base family of colors, you should use brushes for these colors and set them aside strictly for that purpose.

60. It is necessary to apply some type of sealer to preserve stain work.

61. Sealing stain work allows you to use a damp rag for dusting and cleaning without damaging your piece.

62. Sealers for stains are available in matte, semi-gloss or gloss finish and come in either spray-can or in brush-on form.

All Types of Glazes

63. During the glazing process, you may notice some pinholes appearing. To avoid any problems after the piece is fired, be sure to take the end of your brush and work your glaze into the holes.

64. To help the soil in your plants breathe a little more, only glaze the bottom 2-3" up the sides of each pot. This will allow your plants to grow better.

65. If a piece that you have coated with clear glaze comes out of the kiln with a cloudy appearance, you may be applying your glaze too heavily or not firing hot enough. Most times you can correct this fault by firing the piece again at one cone hotter.

66. Crawled glaze is a condition caused by spots on the bisque that are not covered with glaze. This may be from too heavy an application of glaze, oil from the skin left on the piece or hard spots from polishing the greenware. Often the re-application of glaze over these spots and refiring will take care of the problem.

67. To avoid pitting and pinholes in your glaze, be sure that your greenware is free of dust before applying glaze. A damp sponge will help to do the job.

68. Because matte glazes do not flow during the firing process, it is necessary to not only apply them as evenly as possible, but it is also a good idea to rub each coat of color lightly with your fingertips to even out brush strokes and eliminate any glaze pile up.

69. To get glaze to adhere to a porcelain piece, it is necessary to use high-fire glaze

70. Woodtone glazes are best applied with a stiff bristled brush. You can use a variety of brush styles but the key is to brush glaze only in one direction, working out the streaks. Rub each dried coat of color with fingertips to smooth out brush strokes.

71. Another method of taking care of those pinholes on flat surfaces after glazing is to go over the piece with a brush loaded with clear water.

72: If you find it necessary to glaze an already fired piece again, place it in your warm kitchen oven just long enough to get the piece slightly warm. Take the piece out and glaze immediately. The glaze will dry instantly and not slide off the fired surface.

73. Be sure to save those little dabs of glaze left over in a jar. You can pour the excess in a larger jar and save it for later. You probably would not want to use it as a decoration after mixing all the colors together, but you can use it inside of something such as a flower pot where it will not be seen.

74. To remove glaze from the bottom of pieces that you want to dryfoot, mount a piece of sandpaper on a board or table top and simply rub off the glaze in that area.

75. It is never advised, but if you find it necessary to clear glaze over an unfired underglaze or one-stroke, be sure to roll the glaze on, rather than striking with the brush. This will help to avoid smears.

76. A lead pencil is a handy tool for keeping track of the number of coats of glaze you have on a piece. You can write which step you are on over the glaze and the marks will fire away.

77. If you have trouble with red glazes, you might find it helpful to know that this glaze may not act normally if fired with certain other glazes or greenware.

78. Since a satin glaze is one with a soft sheen which moves only slightly during firing, you may be able to create your own by applying alternate coats of transparent matte and a colored gloss glaze.

79. By firing a piece a second time, you can create different effects with your antique, art and some specialty glazes.

80. For best results in glazing, be sure to load brush well with color.

81. Glaze starvation results when a piece does not have adequate color coverage. To correct, simply heat piece in oven, re-apply more glaze and fire again.

82. Did you know that art glazes separate into two or more colors when fired but do not contain crystals? No two pieces are alike.

83. Antique glazes give your pieces a frosted type finish with a variation of two to three shades of the same color. This effect is good for all types of pieces.

84. Did you know that textured glazes (called brocades, flairs, etc.) can be used in combination with most other glazes?

85. Textured glazes can be used for a variety of techniques when used over one-strokes or underglazes.

86. Bubbled glaze can be caused by immature bisque, too heavy an application of color or a kiln that has been fired too rapidly. To correct this fault, grind down the bubbles and high places, add a thin coat of glaze and refire to a cone hotter than originally fired.

87. Cloudy transparent glazes may be caused by too heavy an application of glaze or by not firing the piece hot enough. Correct this by firing piece to one cone hotter.

88. Crackle glazes are formulated to produce those patterns of tiny cracks. To control the amount of cracking, use a thin coat of glaze for a small pattern and for a large pattern a heavy coat of glaze. Bisque must be fired to cone 06.

89. Delayed crazing refers to the period of time that a crackle glaze continues to crack. This effect can last for months.

90. The effect of cracks that appear in glaze that are unwanted is called crazing and may be caused from an under-fired clay body. Bisque should be fired one to two cones hotter than your glaze firing except for those glazes calling for a special firing.

91. If you have a lot of pieces that you want to glaze, you can try the dipping method. There are special glazes designed for this which are concentrated to cover in one coat.

92. Although most glazes are fired in the 05-06 cone range always check the jar for the cone recommended by the manufacturer.

93. If you want to remove the glaze from the bottom of a piece to avoid slippage from stilts during firing, or you plan to felt bottoms, try removing the excess glaze with a piece of window screen placed on a table. Many keep a piece tacked to the corner of their work table at all times just for this purpose.

94. Did you know that flux is added to glazes to reduce the speed and maturing temperature of glazes during firing?

95. Those little chunks of color that are found in crystal glazes are called frit. They are pieces of dried glaze.

96. If you have a problem with glazes coming out with a grainy surface, you may be applying them too thin. The best way to correct this is to warm piece slightly and apply another coat, then refire to proper cone.

97. You can get greyed red or orange family glazes by firing your pieces too hot. Temperature should be at a 06-07 cone.

98. Greyed red family glazes can be caused by not applying enough color. Most manufacturers recommend 4-5 coats.

99. Another cause of greyed red glazes occurs during the firing. They can turn grey if fired with glazes in the yellow, black or green family, or with greenware.

100. Did you know that an opalescent glaze has a milky, translucent, sometimes bluish sheen?

101. Did you know that maturity in ceramics when referring to glazes is the point at which they reach their maximum hardness during the firing process?

102. It is possible to use glazes in an air-brush but they must be watery thin and strained well. Good coverage will require a number of coats. Be sure to apply evenly to avoid runs.

103. If you have trouble getting glaze pieces to set correctly on those star shaped stilts, try using the bar type. You can put them in rows and there will be more points to support the piece.

104. Texture-type glazes may be used in combination with other type glazes. It is possible to create a raised design over a satin glaze since it moves very little in firing.

105. Most people have a favorite brush for applying glazes. However, almost any soft bristle brush will work. Normally they are at least ¾" wide and range up to the "mop" style.

106. For a little different technique you can use sand in combination with your glazes. It should be of a washed, fine grain and can produce a texture if applied to a piece with glaze.

107. If there are certain areas that you do not want to glaze or you do not want colors to overlap, you may have difficulty if not applied properly. Many leave 1/8-3/8" between colors if they do not want them to run together.

108. Most manufacturers recommend that you apply glazes with three coats. There are some one and two coat glazes so be sure to check labels.

109. It is possible to create a third color by mixing two different colored glazes together. It is advisable, however, to fire a sample chip after mixing to be sure that you have the color you want.

110. When applying crystal glazes, it is usually recommended first that you do not mix or stir the jar of color. The first two coats of color should be taken from the top part of jar that contains few crystals. The third and last coat should be applied by dipping into the bottom of the jar, picking up crystals on the brush, and applying to a piece.

111. The size of crystals in a crystal glaze will determine the amount of color variation. The larger the crystals, the more variation of color.

112. If, when you remove a piece of ware from the kiln, it has a lot of streaks or running of glaze to the point where it is dripping off the bottom of the piece, you have applied too much glaze.

113. After you have used glazes a few times, you will discover if you fall in the "light" or "heavy" glaze category. Everyone loads their brush differently and you should know your own tendency so you can gauge how much glaze to apply.

114. For special effects, you can control how the crystals will run on a piece by actually placing them in certain locations. If, for example, you want the crystals to run down only from the top rim of a piece, simply apply the normal number of coats of glaze and add just enough crystals around the top rim to obtain the desired effect.

115. The beauty of a crackle glaze is to create that old look with the cracks. After the piece has set for a few days, coat the entire piece with a dark translucent stain and let dry. Then wipe off with a mineral spirit soaked rag. Only the cracks will hold color, accenting your piece and making it look like an antique.

116. Glazes are easy to use and produce excellent results if applied and fired properly.

117. Did you know that froth is a type of glaze that when fired will produce a foam appearance? It is commonly used to simulate snow.

118. Froth or foam is available from manufacturers in a variety of colors or you can tint it yourself with one-strokes. It can be used to create a lava effect, snow, or a variety of effects. The heavier the coat you apply, the more bubbled and foamy it will be.

119. The type of glazes we use in hobby ceramics fall under the "low-fire" category since the kiln only uses the medium temperature ranges to mature the glazes.

120. Did you know that Majolica is the technique of painting over opaque glazes? Also refers to opaque tinted glazed ware.

121. An opacifier is a material that causes a transparent glaze to become opaque.

122. You may find that glazes are peeling from your ware. This is usually caused by too heavy an application of glaze over underglazes or one-strokes.

123. If, after firing, you have marks in the glaze where the piece rested on a stilt, you can remove these with a rubbing stone. An electric grinding wheel may also be used.

124. It's hard to tell the difference between matte and semi-matte glazes, but the semi-matte glazes have a slightly higher sheen.

125. When using textured glazes, be sure that you are applying the proper number of coats. If you do not apply enough, or if you overfire your piece, the texture you wanted will be almost smooth.

126. Like the name implies, speckle glazes produce just that effect. In the application of the color, you will note little specks or crystals that are applied in each coat of glaze. When fired, these specks produce a varied effect, often called oatmeal.

127. When using woodtone glazes, be sure to brush out the specks you find in the glaze. These specks, when broken and brushed on (all in one direction), will create a wood grain effect.

128. If you have trouble remembering the finished result of a glaze, you can make your own sample chip chart for home use.

129. All glazes need to be fired to maturity to achieve the desired results.

130. Remember that glazes run when fired so you will want to leave your coats of color approximately 1/16-1/8" up from the bottom of the piece.

131. Some glazes do flow more than other

131. Some glazes do flow more than others during firing, but it is impossible as a beginner to know which ones do and don't. You will have to rely on the knowledge of your teacher.

132. Black paste shoe polish can be used to accent the cracks in crackle glazes.

133. Glazes are a formulatin of minerals, watern and other chemicals.

134. Whatever the number of coats, glazes should be applied to your ware in a flowing manner, being sure that you cover your pieces well and evenly.

135. Before applying second and third coats of color, be sure that previous coats have dried completely.

136. It is best to apply glaze in a cross-hatch fashion to eliminate missing any areas.

137. Since clear glaze is the most frequently used and it is often hard to tell which coat you are on, it is possible to color it with food coloring and use a different color for each coat.

138. Glaze that has thickened can be thinned to the proper consistency with the addition of water.

139. Gloss glazes produce a shiny glass-like finish.

140. As the name implies, transparent glazes will allow color to show through, but in the process diffuses them.

141. It is important that you do not over-apply transparent glazes since too much color will give a milky finish over colors.

142. The best method of application of transparent glazes is to thin glaze with water so it is just slightly thicker than water itself and apply recommended number of coats.

143. Semi-matte or satin glazes are opaque in nature and produce very little antiquing or highlighting effects.

144. The best method of applying semi-matte or satin glazes is to thin the first coat of color before applying, which will help eliminate pinholes.

145. It is a good idea to smooth coats of semi-matte or satin glazes with finger tips between coats.

146. Matte glazes produce a dull finish and are opaque in nature.

147. Matte glazes do not flow during firing and must be applied evenly.

148. Brush marks will show when a matte glaze is fired, so be sure to smooth each coat of color with fingertips before applying the next.

149. When using speckle glazes, be sure to stir the jar thoroughly to guarantee the specks will be distributed throughout the glaze.

150. Antique glazes will produce from two to three shades of the same color.

151. Antique glazes are best applied to pieces with good detail that are not too fine or shallow.

152. It is possible to apply antique glazes too thinly, which will eliminate the frosted look.

153. Art glazes produce a finish within themselves during the firing process.

154. Art glazes are formulated to break into a multi-colored effect during the firing process produced by the runs during firing.

155. Because runs are the basis of art glazes, application of the first coat should cover the entire piece. Succeeding applications should be only ¼" from the bottom of the piece.

156. Crackle glazes are for decoration only and are not recommended for use on food or any container that will be exposed to water.

157. It is advisable not to apply a crackle glaze on a piece that has another type of glaze on it too. When fired, there will be two different expansion rates and this may cause pieces to break.

158. Do not use a crackle glaze on the outside of a piece if another type of glaze is being used inside.

159. Crackle glasses are available in a variety of colors and may be in matte,

gloss or transparent varieties.

160. Contrary to most other glazes, crackle glazes only require two coats in application.

161. Crackle glazes may have a tendency to drag when applied, but can be smoothed out with a coating of water on your brush after applying.

162. The cracking effect of a crackle glaze begins to develop even before you remove pieces from the kiln and will continue long afterwards.

163. If, after several months, you notice that you have more cracks in a piece that have not been filled with antiquing when using a crackle glaze, you can go back over the piece to accent them.

164. Woodtone glazes produce finishes similar to wood colors and are quite thick, almost jelly-like in consistency.

165. Woodtone glazes are supposed to be thick in the jar and should not be thinned with water.

166. Woodtone glazes must be applied evenly but not too heavily. Each coat should be smoothed with fingers to avoid bubbling.

167. As you apply each coat of woodtone glaze, it must be thoroughly brushed out into a thin layer.

168. When applying woodtone glazes, the pressure you apply on each brush stroke makes the small dark specks in the glaze dissolve and become dark streaks, which in turn become wood grain when fired.

169. When applying woodtones, be sure that all brush strokes are in the same direction.

170. On highly detailed pieces you may need to thin woodtone glazes slightly to get the specks to form the wood grain effect in the crevices.

171. Don't worry about overbrushing woodtone glazes. The brushing will help to streak and form the wood grain better.

172. Metallic glazes flow quite a bit during firing so the first coat is the only all-over coverage, followed by the last two which should be 1/4" up from the bottom of the piece.

173. Metallic glazes are water soluable and may be thinned with water to ease application.

174. The metallic family of glazes are marketed under a variety of names, but the term defines those colors that contain metallic particles which flow into detailed areas to form shimmering designs.

175. When firing metallic glazes, you get better results by firing them one cone hotter than other glazes and allowing a longer soaking period.

176. During the formulation of red glazes, there are certain minerals hard for manufacturers to eliminate. One of these is manganese which produces a black speck in the finished piece.

177. Black specks in red glazes can also be caused by dirty bisque so be sure to inspect pieces before applying reds.

178. To get the best results with reds, you should apply glazes of the same family on bisque.

179. Red glazes should not be thinned when applying three coats of even coverage. Some teachers even recommend four to five coats.

180. Most of the problems with red glazes occur during the firing process.

181. The recommended bisque you should use for red glazes is that which has been fired to cone 04 or 05.

182. You should not fire raw clay bodies with reds.

183. Glazes must be used on anthing that will contain water.

184. Salt from your hands when sweating or even the lead shavings from a pencil will effect red glazes.

185. Textured glazes are that family of colors that produce special surfaces when fired.

186. Textured glazes are often so coarse they appear to be a gravel or stucco finish.

187. Any glaze may be used over embossing glaze as long as the embossing glaze has been fired first.

188. Embossing glazes are opaque and, if used in too wide an area, can crack in the firing.

189. Embossing glazes do not flow in the firing process.

190. The easiest way to apply crystal glazes is to begin by not mixing the jar of color. Pour off the majority of the glaze on the top of the jar, which will be glaze without crystals. Apply the first two coats of color from this supply. Let dry and apply the remaining glaze and crystals.

191. You should take care not to apply crystals from crystal glazes too near the bottom of a piece to avoid drippings and puddles on the bottom of pieces.

192. The effects you achieve with crystal glazes will never be the same on two different pieces.

193. The label "lead safe" does not necessarily mean that a glaze contains no lead, but it does meet minimum government standards for dinnerware items.

194. A lead-free glaze means that it contains no lead at all.

195. Spill base is that class of glaze that is applied over, under or between application of other colored glazes, causing them to blend and form spill effects when fired.

196. Pattern base is a special effect glaze that will cause glazes to separate during the firing and form varied patterns.

Molds and Pouring

197. When pouring small molds, you may sometimes experience difficulty in getting the slip to drain from small pour holes. Try using an atomizer with a piece of small flexible tubing attached. Insert tube into the pour hole, turn mold over, and pump air into the mold. The slip will then run out freely.

198. To release greenware that sticks to a mold, use your airbrush.

199. To avoid a poor fit on pieces that have lids, be sure to place lids on bottoms and allow them to dry together. Even if you should accidently mis-shape the piece, the lid will still fit.

200. To repair a mold that has a piece chipped out of it, use evaporated milk instead of glue. It makes a perfect bond.

201. If you have a mold line that is difficult to remove from a piece of greenware, dampen the piece slightly. It will come off easier and lessen the chance of breaking the piece.

202. Did you know that "cases" are the frames around a block used in the formation of ceramic molds?

203. Are you having difficulty getting that last bit of slip drained from a mold? Try using a meat baster with a rubber bulb and suck it out. A medicine dropper also works, but is much slower and harder to clean.

204. You can make various sizes of earrings by pouring slip into the various sized keys in your molds.

205. When casting cups, glasses or other pieces that have round openings, use old discarded light bulbs of various sizes inserted inside to keep them round.

206. Next time you strain slip, use a piece of women's hose rather than a sieve.

207. You can make your own color chip chart just like your local studio has by using small inexpensive molds and pouring your own chips.

208. It is important not to dry your molds too fast. Store them on slated shelves so the natural air can circulate around them well.

209. When buying a new mold be sure you always open it immediately to inspect the inside for any damage.

210. When cleaning the inside of a mold, never use anything other than a brush. If you encounter a stubborn piece of clay simply roll some waste clay into a ball and pounce it out.

211. Since molds work on the principal of absorption, it is important that you avoid touching the inside with your fingers. You do not want to leave any oil residue that may clog pores.

212. Be sure that you remove all dried clay from the seam area of a mold. It can dry and when you put the mold back together and start pouring again, the dried clay may warp the mold and eventually cause it to leak.

213. Ideally, molds should not touch each other when you are storing and/or drying them.

214. Never store molds directly on metal shelves. The moisture from within the molds will condense on them and cause rust spots on your molds.

215. You may notice a fuzz on your molds when they are being stored. This fuzz is caused by deflocculents in the slip that have penetrated the mold. You should remove this fuzz as it will harden and plug the pores of the mold.

216. Never put a wet mold on top of a kiln to dry. The uneven heat may cause the mold to warp.

217. If you must force-dry a mold do it in front of a forced-air electric beater. It should not be too close. If it is too close to hold your hand in that spot, it is too close for the mold. Turn mold frequently.

218. If you live in an area where bees, bugs, wasps, etc. might build a nest in your stored molds, be sure to cover the pour holes.

219. The terms pour hole or pour gate mean the same thing.

220. When pouring cups, be sure to lie the mold with the handle down after draining, so any excess slip will fill the handle and avoid leaving a bacteria trap.

221. The simplest mold to cast is the one-piece variety. There is no need to band it. It is easily drained and, in most instances, the casting comes free without difficulty.

222. When stirring your slip, use a round dowel. This is less likely to cause air bubbles.

223. Slip should be about the consistency of heavy cream for proper pouring.

224. Many people put several layers of newspaper on the table before pouring to make the clean-up easier. Rolling up the top layer usually takes care of any spills.

225. If the thickness of your slip is about 3/16" in the mold, it is about ready to be drained unless you want a particularly thick piece.

226. After draining a mold be sure to set it back upright to prevent the formation of nipples or lumps on the bottom surface.

227. When removing a piece from the mold be careful not to deform it in moving or to scratch it with your fingernails.

228. Some one-piece molds do not need to be drained. These are very shallow molds which can be cast by pressing modeling clay or by pouring slip and letting it set until solid.

229. Two-piece molds come in two types. Some have the seam line on the finished casting running vertically and some horizontally.

230. It is important that you use enough straps or bands to hold the pieces of your mold together to prevent leakage.

231. Always pour slip in such a way that the initial contact of slip to mold is in a place that isn't critical, such as the bottom. At this point the silicates build up and may cause hard spots in your bisque that will not take decorations properly.

232. One method of avoiding a hard or "hot spot" when pouring, is to insert a tongue depressor or other flat object in the mold and pour your slip against it.

233. A simple way to drain those molds with small pour holes is to insert a soda straw and blow in it as you drain the mold. The straw acts as a vent allowing air in to displace the slip.

234. Always cut the spare or pour ring from your mold rather than tearing it off. Tearing can cause undue stress and may result in a crack.

235. Casting a box is like any other casting with the exception that you must end up with a lid that fits.

236. After taking a box and its lid out of the mold, put the two together and allow them to dry. This will insure a proper fit.

237. It is possible to use condensed milk to glue the parts together if your broken mold is fairly small and the break clean, without too much chipping. Pieces must fit together smoothly to use this repair method.

238. It is possible to mend broken molds with glue but you must be careful not to get any glue in the mold. If any does spill onto the face of the casting area, be sure to remove it with fine sandpaper so the pores will not be clogged.

239. If a mold suddenly starts leaking after it's about half full, you probably didn't band it tightly enough.

240. If you know a mold is going to leak ahead of time, you can stop it by damming the leak with a piece of damp clay.

241. Before casting a multiple-piece mold, take it apart and examine it so you will know which piece should be removed first after the slip has been poured and the greenware is ready to be removed.

242. To help you remember the disassembling order in a multiple-piece mold, use a waterproof felt tip pen to number the pieces.

243. If there is something special that you must know about a particular mold before casting it, such as "Drain With Straw", etc., mark the outside of the mold with a waterproof felt tip pen.

244. Once you have examined a new mold for any breakage and are ready to pour, look it over one more time to see if it has any special problems you will have to cope with such as a small pour hole, undercuts, tricky draining, etc.

245. If a mold has two pour holes on opposite sides, lumps may form on the bottom while the other side is being poured. It might work well to pour the top of a piece first since cone-shaped tops usually don't make lumps.

246. Heavy seams on greenware can be the result of not banding your molds tightly enough.

247. If pieces collapse when removed from the mold, try putting a foam rubber piece inside of the greenware and nesting them in shredded paper to dry.

248. Cracks around the pour hole of a greenware piece are commonly caused by tearing, rather than cutting, the spare off and may only appear after firing.

249. A mold is like any other tool in that it will wear out after prolonged use.

250. If you have poured a mold a number of times and it shows wear it is possible to scribe some of the detail back by carefully carving with a sharp tool.

251. Molds are expensive and should be cared for properly like any other investment.

252. Soft spots in greenware are usually caused by mold contamination from body oils, wax or even mold releases.

253. Pieces which explode in the kiln are generally the result of improper venting or improper draining of greenware.

254. Indented vertical lines are usually caused on the greenware by "drizzling" slip down the sides of a vase or pitcher. They can be repaired, most of the time, by painting thickened slips into them and smoothing with a damp sponge.

255. If a plate or bowl separates into two layers, either you opened the mold too soon or you drained it too soon.

256. Air bubbles (pin holes) in greenware can come from air in the slip from stirring too briskly or pouring too rapidly.

257. Air bubbles on rims of pieces can be reduced by rocking the mold while pouring.

258. Tiles or stick-ons which seem solid may blister or explode in the kiln.

259. Narrow stick-ons or small castings which are incomplete may be caused by too thick slip.

260. Objects cracking in the mold result from leaving the casting in the mold too long. Shrinkage causes cracking.

261. A gang mold is what the name implies, a gang of molds made into one. Chess sets are usually gang molds.

262. Core molds are similar to gang molds except that they have only one pour gate that branches inside the mold.

263. Double casting is a two (or more) color casting technique using multiple colors of slip.

264. Be sure that the spouts of tea pots are not solid. To see if it is, blow gently through it after you drain the mold.

265. Keep the table where you band your molds and the bands themselves as clean as possible to prevent bits of dried slip and trash from falling into the molds as you band them.

266. If you band your molds with the pour gate down, it will help to keep the inside cavity clean.

267. If you have a new mold that sticks together and, no matter what you do, will not open, try saturating the seam area all around with water by pouring it right on the mold. Then go ahead and cast it in your normal manner and it should open easily.

268. Did you know that a "block" is the reverse impression of a finished ceramic mold, usually made of hydrocal or rubber? Plaster impressions of this block are taken that become your casting mold.

269. Leatherhard means that the greenware has dried to the point where it is firm but not void of visual water.

270. A mold is like any tool. You take care of it and it will always be there to help you do a job.

Brushes

271. A ceramist's best friend are her brushes!!! Give them good care and they will servie you well.

272. Use a piece of styrofoam to stick the tips of handles in with bristles up to store brushes.

273. Brushes may be washed in soap and water as long as they are rinsed clean before use with a particular media.

274. Never store brushes so that bristles are bent backward or out of shape.

275. Wet your brush before applying glaze or underglaze. Never wet a brush before applying metallics, translucent stains, lustres or your mother-of-pearls.

276. If you have some difficulty in getting some of the sticky gum material out of your brushes, try dipping them in nail polish remover (banana oil) and wiping clean. Be sure to rinse well with water afterwards.

277. When painting areas that are hard to get at, take an old brush and bend the metal part with a pair of pliers to reach around corners.

278. Brush hairs will fire out of gloss glaze, but will not fire out of underglaze, matte, semi-matte or satin glazes.

279. When cleaning brushes, always use a two-bottle wash. Use the first to clean your brush as well as you can, then do a final cleaning in a clean second jar. When the first jar becomes too dirty, move your second up to first and get a new second. Let the first jar of cleaner settle and pour off the clean solvent or thinner for using again.

280. Did you know that "hard hair" refers to brushes that have stiff bristles.?

281. Did you know that having a camel hair brush does not mean that your brush is made from the hair of a camel? It refers to a type of soft hair used in making the brush, with squirrel hair being the finest.

282. Did you know that "sabeline" is a specially prepared ox hair that is used in brushes?

283. A brush kit is usually a selection of three or more brushes combined into one group and is usually designed for a specific purpose.

284. Feather stroking is a painting technique of using thinned paint about the consistency of milk with a flat brush. Short strokes are taken across a paper towel to split brush hairs for color application.

285. The ferrule is the metal band toward the end of the brush that holds the bristles together.

286. A liner is a long bristled brush used for design work.

287. Double-load is the term that applies to loading your brush with more than one color. The load can be increased to three or four colors.

288. As with any tool, the better quality you buy, the better and easier the job becomes. The same applies to brushes. The higher priced brushes are worth their cost.

289. Your stain brushes, made of stiff white bristles, will become stained when used in a variety of colors. This does not mean there is still paint in them.

290. Never let your brushes stand in water or other cleaner even if you are going to use them right away. This will tend to bend the bristles and may cause them to stay that way permanently.

291. When cleaning your brushes, never push the bristles against the bottom of the container that holds the cleaner. The bristles could be cut off when you bend them back over the metal ferruel.

292. If you know that you are not going to be using a particular brush for a long period of time, it is best to dampen it in glycerine or soap, form a point or flat edge as applies and let it dry. This will act as sizing and insure that your bristles will be the right shape when you are ready to use them. Simply wash them out before using. using.

293. The trick to most brush strokes is holding the brush correctly. It is best not to hold it like a pencil but rather between the thumb and forefinger.

294. A dime store brush will produce dime store results.

295. Ever wonder why brushes are so expensive? Think of all the little hairs that have to go into one brush and the price of high quality fur which they come from. In addition, all quality brushes are hand made.

296. Remember, a brush acts like a fountain pen, allowing color to flow down the brush body to the tip as you work.

297. Hold your brush as straight up and down as you can, using light pressure when you are making lines.

299. Proper care of brushes will make them last almost forever.

298. If brushes do not come as clean as you want when cleaning in water, you can run them under the faucet. You may also wash brushes in mild detergent as long as you wash out the soap when done.

300. Practice makes perfect when learning brush strokes. Experiment a bit of applying different pressure to your brush tip to learn the effects different pressures have.

301. When using your brush the more pressure you exert, the fatter the lines will be and the more color you will lay down.

302. When loading your brush you should remember that you do not load a dry brush. When using water base colors, always dampen the bristles first before loading with color.

303. When loading a liner brush, emerse the bristles entirely in color. Pull the brush through the color, turning the brush at the same time, so your bristles form a fine point. Do not put too much pressure on the brush when doing this or you will squeeze out all the color.

304. To load a square shader, emerse it in color by pulling it through the color. After it is loaded, press both sides of the tip of the brush flat against your palette to form a sharp edge.

305. You may build depth in your shading strokes by laying different colors over each other. This is done by stroking the darkest color on the bottom and applying a lighter color over the top.

306. To build depth with a brush stroke, you can double-load your brush with two different colors. This is usually done by loading your brush with the lightest color and tipping in a darker color. Then stroke on the color. The action of the brush will inter-mix colors. You should not try to get too many strokes out of one brush load however. Celan your brush and start again about every 2-3 strokes.

Overglazes

307. If you want a brighter fired gold, you might try applying it over yellow instead of clear glaze.

308. Before applying gold or any metallics, clean area with alcohol. All areas should be dry before painting with bright gold or other overglazes.

309. Some people use saliva to remove unfired gold.

310. If you plan to cover a large area with liquid bright gold, you may have to thin it a bit in a small dish before applying.

311. Do you have a green glaze that won't take a gold firing? Try firing it at a higher or lower temperature than your usual gold fire (cones 018-022).

312. Brushing is the most popular method of application but liquid bright gold, as well as other overglazes, may be applied with a brush, sponge, spray, stamp or almost any other method to secure the desired finish.

313. If in firing your lustres, crystals appear, it usually indicates too much heat. However, if a lustre is too old, the same condition may also appear.

314. If overglazes are applied to a textured surface and they fire off the raised areas, but fire perfectly in the recessed areas, this usually indicates an over-application of color. The weight of the material applied pulled itself off and into the recessed areas.

315. Thin, even applications of lustres and metallics are necessary. If a deeper color is desired then re-apply and refire.

316. Never patch a spot with overglazes. Go back over the entire area and refire.

317. After using a marbleizing liquid with metallics, there is a residue that remains on a piece. It can easily be removed with soap and water.

318. Never use a brush that has been used to apply a water base product to apply a solvent or oil-based product such as lustre.

319. Over a typical, ceramic glaze, lustres and metallics are fired to cone 018-019. There are a few exceptions so be sure to check the product you are using.

320. When working with lustres, all forms of contamination must be avoided. The work area and object must be free of dust, dirt, and moisture.

321. Halo Gold, Halo Platinum or Halo Copper firing purple, brown, or blue is caused by too light a color of glaze. In order for these metallics to work, they must be applied over a darker glaze.

322. When using a brush to apply overglazes, it is best accomplished with the largest brush suitable to the object being decorated.

323. Ventilation is the key to satisfactory firing of metallics and lustres. The kiln should remain open until all smoke and odor have ceased.

324. Halo lustres and metallics can never be thinned since the solvents in these products must be present in exact proportions. Every effort must be made to insure little evaporation.

325. For a special technique, you can overfire a metallic. Fire it hotter than normal and the glaze will begin to move, making the overglaze move as well as developing voids that allow the color of the glaze to show through.

326. Proper overglaze decorating begins with the greenware. Greenware which is to be overglazed should be carefully cleaned and fired to cone 04.

327. You can apply gold using a pen designed for that purpose.
drop at a time to avoid over thinning.

328. In firing an overglaze, the glaze is softened to the point where the overglaze settles onto the softened surface and becomes a part of that surface.

329. Overfiring an overglaze will cause colors to sink too deeply into the glaze resulting in distortion, fade-out or burn-out.

330. Overglaze refers to the group of colors which are applied to a previously glazed and fired surface.

331. The best known of the overglaze decorations is liquid bright gold which is a true solution of gold in solvents and oils.

332. Brushes used for lustres and metallics should be kept thoroughly clean and protected from contamination between uses.

333. The object to which you are applying the overglaze must be thoroughly clean. Use a lint-free cloth and alcohol as the cleaner.

334. If you use alcohol to clean pieces before applying overglazes, be sure to allow plenty of drying time before starting to apply color.

335. If you want to use a sponge to apply an overglaze, allow the lustre or metallic to thicken slightly by exposing a small amount to the air and allowing a little evaporation. The thickened material will hold the sponge pattern after application.

336. White spots, or spots of glaze color showing through your overglaze, are caused by moisture present on the object when the overglaze was applied.

337. Cracked metal overglazes are caused by firing to an excessive temperature.

338. If you remove a piece from the kiln that you applied liquid bright gold to and it rubs off the piece, it has been underfired.

339. If a piece removed from the kiln that has had gold applied has hair-line cracks, it has been overfired.

340. An unusual effect can be achieved by applying mother-of-pearl lustre with finger tips in a swirling motion. Be sure hands are clean.

341. To remove unfired lustre that is smudged or messy, use rubbing alcohol.

342. If you are having trouble with purple spots on your pieces that you want gold or lustres on, try wearing gloves when applying.

343. Overglazes may be thinned with essence (gold essence for metallics, lustre essence for lustres). Add essence one drop at a time to avoid overthinning.

344. Lustres and metallics can be applied by rubber stamping.

345. Since there is a great similarity between unfired metallics and lustres, it is important that you keep your containers labeled well for identification.

346. Proper brush technique is important in overglaze decorating. The brush should be well saturated but with the excess material worked out. Each stroke should

be firmly and evenly placed next to the last one.

347. Cloudy or dull lustres or metallics may be caused by insufficient ventilation or firing to an excessive temperature.

348. Water is the enemy of overglazes.

349. Poor adherence of overglazes to an object can be caused by poor ventilation, insufficient temperature, or contamination on the ware.

350. Brushes you use for overglazes should not be cleaned in alcohol, since inner bristles will tend to hold part of the water that is contained in alcohol.

351. You have heard it before, but coughing, sneezing and cigarette smoke can also put moisture on an object that is to be overglazed and may cause an imperfection.

352. It is a good idea to set aside a specific brush for a certain type of overglaze. Mark each brush as to what they were used for and save them for that purpose.

353. Speed is necessary when applying lustres. They dry very fast and if you take too long, they could dry, forming rings which would be unattractive.

354. If you are not satisfied that you have applied the proper and even coverage, you can use lacquer thinner on a rag to remove the lustre and start over.

355. Lustres can be used in a spray bottle or airbrush. It is necessary to follow cleanliness procedures and practice to get the proper coverage.

356. It is best not to fire lustres with china paints as the turpentine in china paints may distort your lustres.

357. When loading your kiln with pieces that have overglazes, be sure to leave plenty of room between pieces and do not cut off ventilation to the bottom pieces by covering them with a full shelf.

358. During the firing process of overglazes, strong fumes are generated in the evaporation of oils. Be sure the room is well ventilated as the smell may be irritating to many of your friends, family or even yourself.

359. If your glaze surface has pinholes or other faults it will effect the finished overglaze.

360. Do not work in areas where there is a strong draft when applying overglazes. The breeze may blow dust on the piece you are adding overglaze to or to one that is drying.

361. A black or white speck in your overglaze after it has been fired may be caused by dust.

362. If you want a deeper color of overglaze, don't try a thick application to do the job. Apply normally and fire, then apply another coat and refire.

363. If a spot or blemish does appear on your overglazed piece when removed, do not try to patch it. Cover the entire piece with another application of color and refire.

364. It is important that you always keep one brush soley for mother-of-pearl lustre and use it for nothing else. You can use the same brush for some other overglazes as long as it is thoroughly cleaned between different color uses.

365. When applying lustres to a textured surface, be sure to brush out the excess overglaze from the crevices while it is still wet and can be seen. If you do not it will burn off in these recessed areas during firing.

366. Lustres and metallics do have a suspension agent and are subject to evaporation. This is why there are thinners that can be added to them a drop at a time to get them back to proper painting consistency.

367. When loading your brushes in preparation to applying overglaze, do not dip your brush into the overglaze all the way up to the metal ferrule. This only wastes color and makes brushes difficult to clean.

368. You can apply opal or mother-of-pearl lustres over a fired coat of another lustre or metallic.

369. Lustres and metallics take on the surface texture of glazes they are applied over. Satin or matte glazes will yield a dull finish and gloss glaze will yield a shiny finish.

370. Underfiring an overglaze will prevent the glaze from becoming soft enough to receive the color, thus causing poor adherence.

371. You may use more than one overglaze on a piece but they should be fired between applications.

372. The normal color of gold and lustres is oil brown when applied.

373. A proper finish of opal and Mother-of-Pearl lustre can be guaranteed with a light application.

374. Unlike other lustres and metallics, opal and mother-of-pearl should be applied unevenly. This is best accomplished by swirling or stippling with the brush during application.

375. Pieces that have overglazes applied to them should be allowed to dry in an area free from contamination by smoke, dust, dirt or moisture before firing.

376. Blistering or flaking of a lustre is caused by too heavy an application.

377. Areas of purple, blue or brown on metallic coatings are caused by too light an application of the metallic overglaze.

378. Overglazes should be allowed to dry 24 hours before firing.

379. When an even edge is required or when it is being applied to a raised or embossed surface, an overglaze may be allowed to thicken slightly.

380. You can make overglazes thicker by pouring a little in a clean dish and exposing it to the air for a time, allowing a bit of evaporation.

381. When gold comes out of the kiln with purple spots it is usually caused by too thin an application of gold or too much thinner in the overglaze.

382. When firing lustre, do not place the piece to be fired directly on a hot bottom or shelf as the radiation of the heat will drive the lustre away.

383. Pieces to be decorated with overglaze should be at room temperature. Articles from a hot kiln will cause the oils in the overglazes to evaporate.

384. China paints belong to the overglaze family of colors.

385. If an area to be covered with china paints is large enough or does not have too many recessed areas, you may have better luck in applying colors with a "pad".

386. A pad, as referred to in china painting, is a piece of china silk filled with either cotton or lamb's wool and tied together to form a loose ball.

387. Burnished golds are those that must be polished when removed from the kiln.

388. Lustre resist is a product that is used for blocking out areas that you do not want to add lustre to. It fires away.

389. Never dip your brush directly into a container of metallic or lustre to begin application. Always pour a small amount of color into an alcohol cleaned container and load brushes from this. These materials are expensive and you may have a contaminated brush and ruin an entire supply rather than just a bit in a dish.

390. It is possible to remove mistakes when using gold or lustres by using a "gold eraser". It looks like a normal eraser but is chemically formulated to do the job as well as containing and abrasive.

391. The use of metallic overglazes and lustres add a great deal of beauty and value to a piece. It should be noted that a piece is even more beautiful with multiple applications with firings in-between.

392. If you want a multi-colored effect in your mother-of-pearl lustre, it can be accomplished by firing your lustred piece with different colored glazed pieces at the same time.

Porcelain

393. You can help prevent porcelain cups from going out of shape during the firing by kiln washing the rims and placing one cup on top of the other, rims together and handles opposite for balance.

394. The selection of pieces to be cast in porcelain is important. They should be graceful, useful and fire to cone 6 without support.

395. Did you know that porcelain will shrink approximately 15 percent during the firing process?

396. Porcelain slip should always be strained.

397. The consistency of porcelain slip is important in the casting process. It should be the consistency of light cream. If thinning is needed, you should use distilled water.

398. Porcelain pieces are cast approximately one-third thinner than hobby ceramic pieces.

399. When pouring your own porcelain pieces, you must be careful not to pour too many molds at once since porcelain slip sets up much faster than ceramic. Small pieces will be ready to drain in as few as one-two minutes.

400. Unlike ceramics, if a porcelain piece is distorted when being removed from a mold and reshaped, it will go back to the distorted shape during the firing process.

401. If you are a little afraid of handling delicate porcelain greenware, you can fire it to 018 before cleaning.

402. Because porcelain shrinks, it is necessary to do a good job of cleaning the seams off since a ridge will form when fired.

403. A kiln capable of reaching a temperature of 2250 degrees (cone 6) is necessary to fire porcelain.

404. If you do not fire porcelain properly, the various colors that porcelain is available in will not be true.

405. When firing porcelain, your kiln must be very clean. To insure that it is, you should vacuum it out before a porcelain firing.

406. Porcelain pieces cannot be stilted when fired, and pieces cannot touch each other since the high temperature will make them stick together. Your kiln shelves must have an adequate covering of kiln wash as well to keep them from sticking.

407. Porcelain pieces should be kept at least two inches from the side walls or elements of your kiln during firing.

408. Some pieces having overhangs must be fired on a setter or they will sag or collapse during firing.

409. Setters are not used during the glaze firing of porcelain.

410. Pieces of porcelain that have a heavy handle or a overhang must have a support or prop. This can be made from some spare trimmings during the casting. Make sure it is the right height and kiln wash any points that will be touching your pieces.

411. When you remove porcelain pieces from a bisque firing, you will note that they have a slightly rough feeling. Before decorating, polish them with a 100 grit scrubber until you have a soft, satin finish.

412. During the firing process, porcelain becomes vitreous or water tight so there is no need to glaze the inside of pieces.

413. Some clear glazes are not compatible with porcelain and will not take the high temperature. Be sure you check to see if you are using the proper type.

414. Most clear glaze for porcelain is fired to cone 2 or 3.

415. When firing pieces such as a box with lid in porcelain, the two pieces must be fired together to insure a proper fit. Since porcelain becomes almost liquid during firing, it is necessary to coat the touch surfaces with high-fire kiln wash.

416. All porcelain pieces must be dry-footed since they cannot be supported by stilts during a glaze firing. If you should attempt to do so, the stilts would go right through the bottom of the piece.

417. When mixing kiln wash to use as a separating agent for touching porcelain surfaces, it should be mixed 50-50 with water.

418. When firing porcelain, do not place the top of a piece of ware closer than two inches to the lid or an overhead shelf.

419. Because porcelain comes in a variety of colors, it is not necessary to paint a background on porcelain pieces.

420. Lustres or decals may be fired onto a unglazed piece of porcelain bisque.

421. Some decals when fired directly on porcelain bisque will change colors so they should be test-fired before ruining your favorite piece.

422. It is possible to decorate porcelain bisque with underglazes and one-strokes. This has to be done at a soft bisque (018) since porcelain fired to maturity would not absorb the color. Some of these colors change when high-fired so it is best to run tests on colors.

423. You may antique porcelain soft bisque (018) much as you would any other ceramic piece.

424. When draping porcelain dolls, the lace should be washed in advance to remove any sizing.

425. Lace dolls or any draping project should be fired slower and allowed to cool over a longer period of time.

426. You can use the same molds to cast porcelain that you use for ceramics. They must be cleaned quite well, however.

427. A gallon of porcelain slip will produce one-third more pieces than a gallon of ceramic slip.

428. When used with porcelain, molds will have a longer life and produce twice as many castings while remaining cleaner.

429. Cotton lace is the only kind of lace that will work effectively for porcelain draping.

430. In the technique of porcelain lace draping, a piece of cotton lace is saturated with porcelain slip and added to a doll. When the piece is fired the cotton lace burns out leaving a fine shell of porcelain that was in the orginally saturated lace.

431. Plasticizer may be added to porcelain slip to retard the set-up time.

432. It is possible to use porcelain to double cast as well as create the Wedgewood porcelain technique.

One-Strokes
(Translucent Underglazes)

433. You can erase one-stroke from bisque with a rubber eraser.

434. One-strokes must be thinned with water on a tile before application.

435. One-strokes are concentrated color pigments with no clay added and may be translucent or opaque.

436. Soluable in water, one-strokes can be used for washes, outlines and small areas of concentrated color.

437. One-strokes are not recommended for large area coverage. These are concentrated colors and will streak if not applied properly.

438. As the name applies, only one coat of color is required when using one-strokes.

439. One-strokes may be used on either bisque or greenware.

440. Since one-strokes are pure color pigment, the color you see in the jar is the color you will obtain on a finished piece.

441. It is possible to mix two one-stroke colors to make a third. Since they are pure color, you will know immediately if the mixture is the way you want it to be.

442. When thinning your colors to painting consistency with water, the more water you add the thinner and lighter the color will become.

443. If you plan on using only a small amount of a one-stroke color, it is possible to obtain the proper painting consistency by loading a wet brush with color.

444. Darker one-stroke colors usually need more thinning than lighter colors.

445. When using one-strokes you may find that colors look too light after your piece has been fired. This is caused by not applying enough color. If you apply too much however, there is a possibility of it popping off.

446. Do not apply one-stroke by flowing it on like glaze. Simply load your brush properly and apply it in smooth, even strokes.

447. All brush streaks will show when applying one-stroke. Even, smooth coverage is important.

448. If you see some of your strokes streaking when applying one-stroke, go back over them with additional color and smooth them out.

449. By using a combination of water and one-stroke on your brush, you can paint shaded areas in one-stroke, from light to dark.

450. You can apply one-stroke with just about anything to a ceramic piece. Brushes, sponges, fingers, etc., will all work.

451. You can make an antiquing wash using one-stroke by mixing color pigment to about 3 to 4 parts water. The less water, the darker the wash.

452. Using one-stroke for antique effects is best accomplished on bisque.

453. It is possible to decorate with one-stroke over an unfired matte glaze.

454. You can change the color of an opaque underglaze by adding one-stroke to it. You should test fire your new color before using, however.

455. One-strokes can be used to color ceramic slip. It takes quite a bit but you can do it. You may also add it to slip and swirl it in, casting a piece immediately. When fired, the piece will have a marbled effect.

456. One-strokes can be used in combination with embossing glaze by loading brush with glaze, tipping in one-stroke and applying to piece. This is an effective means of creating flower petals.

457. One-strokes may be used to tint embossing glazes.

458. One-strokes can be used to decorate over a sponged-on froth glaze.

459. Solid covered backgrounds with opaque underglazes are most commonly decorated with one-strokes.

460. Since one-strokes are concentrated color pigments, they are most commonly used to write messages or sign pieces that will later be glazed.

461. One-strokes are not sealed media. They must be coated with a transparent or clear glaze.

462. One-strokes that have curled or peeled away from the surface painted over a matte glaze are caused by too heavy an application of color.

463. Streaked or running strokes painted with one-strokes may be caused by attempts to glaze over one-strokes before firing.

464. If one-strokes are too dark after being fired, you may be applying too much color.

465. Loading your brush slightly with one-stroke will allow you to create a dry-brush technique.

466. One-strokes should be thinned about 50-50 with water for use in an airbrush.

467. One-strokes may be used only under transparent matte glaze.

Opaque Underglaze

468. Thin down underglazes with water if they are too thick.

469. When using underglazes, do not back-stroke when applying, as this will cause a pile-up of paint or a pulling off of the paint already applied.

470. Underglazes are designed for all over coverage such as for background work. They are not good for detail work.

471. In most cases three coats are required for using underglazes. Each coat should be applied in opposite directions.

472. Underglazes should be used only on greenware. They can be used on bisque however and fired before a glaze application.

473. Underglazes as we know them, are opaque. They are formulated from color pigment and clay to give solid, opaque coverage.

474. You can apply one color of underglaze over the other. Being opaque, the top color will cover the underlying color completely.

475. Underglazes should be applied to dry greenware. If greenware is still damp when applied, the underglaze colors may chip off after firing.

476. It is possible to polish underglazes in special techniques. The regular three coats are applied, followed by a fourth. Before the fourth is dry, polish with a soft rag to a satin sheen.

477. Unless a special technique is desired, underglazes require a sealing coat of fired glaze.

478. A favorite technique for the use of underglazes is sgrafitto. Apply your normal three coats and let dry. Transfer a pattern to piece and, with a sharp tool, scribe or cut through the underglaze into the greenware. You should slightly dampen lines you are scribing to prevent chipping. When completed, fire as normal, then add covering glaze and fire again. Scribed lines will show white through your underglaze covering.

479. Since underglazes are largely clay, you can use this as a decorating advantage. Combine some ground clay with the application of your underglaze colors and apply three coats. The piece will have texture.

480. The clay and color combination contained in underglazes form a bond with the greenware after being fired.

481. Remember that underglazes are used for wide area coverage.

482. The color in the jar of underglaze is not the resulting color when fired.

483. You can change the color of underglazes with the addition of one-strokes (pure color pigments) in varying quantities. Since you still will not be able to tell the color you have until after the piece is fired, it is recommended to make a test-firing of piece to be sure the color is what you want.

484. Underglazes are poor choices for design work. Since it is necessary to apply three coats for effective coverage, you can see how difficult it would be to make three lines directly on top of each other.

485. It is best to thin down the first coat of underglaze with about two parts color to one of water. This is called a scrub coat. The second and third coats are applied at full strength.

486. It is important to keep your brush loaded when applying underglazes, but you do not want to add color as you would when painting a house.

487. Remember that your colors must be dry before taking any next step, whether it is firing or adding design work over your underglaze base.

Kilns and Firing

488. Glazes and clays mature at different temperatures and may vary from company to company. Always check the container or package for the recommended firing cone.

489. Bisque should be fired at least one cone hotter than glaze.

490. If you are firing pieces such as cups and plates that will be subject to thermal shock (rapid changes in temperature), you should fire them to cone 04.

491. Porcelain is normally fired to cone 5 or 6 and requires a slow firing schedule.

492. You are asking for trouble if you try to speed the cooling process of your kiln and force the temperature down by opening the peep holes or lid too soon. If cooled too rapidly, your pieces may craze or you could possibly do damage to your kiln.

493. If after firing, you discover some black specks in your glaze, it may be caused by the use of dirty brush, greenware, bisque or other tools you have used. Your kiln, if dirty, can cause this as well.

494. Even though your automatic kiln sitter is adjusted at the factory, it may be jarred out of adjustment during shipping or delivery and should be checked again.

495. You can have an overfiring if a piece falls against the sensing rod of your automatic kiln sitter and prevents it from falling.

496. If the rate of temperature rise is slow during firing, a cone may bend at a lower temperature than if the temperature rise is rapid.

497. If you purchase a pyrometer to aid in firing, be sure that you mount it on the wall and not on the kiln, as heat will damage it.

498. If your kiln is equipped with a limit timer as well as an automatic kiln sitter, you should set the timer for about half an hour beyond your expected rising time.

499. A pyrometer is a temperature indicating meter. It can be used to monitor the heating or cooling rate of your kiln. A pyrometer is very valuable when doing glass work or soaking glazes.

500. Glazed ceramic pieces should dry for at least six hours before firing.

501. It is best to fire a piece in its natural position, however, large flat items such as wall plaques or clocks should be fired on a flat side to prevent warpage.

502. When loading your kiln, place your shelves in the kiln carefully so the walls of the kiln will not be bumped and damaged.

503. Do not jar or shake your kiln after the loading has started since the ware on a shelf could be knocked down or broken.

504. Load only bone-dry greenware into your kiln.

505. Wet greenware may crack during firing or explode, resulting in damage to other ware in the kiln.

506. Ceramic greenware should be dried for at least two days, with larger or thicker pieces requiring even longer before firing.

507. Cones are available in different numbers and the user must insure that items being fired are fired to the cone recommended by the manufacturer.

508. An overfiring in your kiln can occur if the kiln sitter is out of adjustment or if the free fall of the weight is impeded.

509. Cones are slender pyramids composed of ceramic materials used to determine the combined effect of temperature and time which is sometimes called "heat work".

510. Clays and glazes are fired to different end points referred to by their cone equivalent or number.

511. To keep flat pieces from warping in bisque firing, lay them flat on two half shelves with a small space between them.

512. A pyrometer should not be used as a substitute for pyrometric cones to determine the maturity of the ware.

513. Glass sagging involves placing of a piece of glass such as a sheet or a bottle in a mold and heating it until the glass softens and takes the shape of the mold.

514. When sagging glass in a mold, be sure to dust the mold with whiting or some recognized separation agent or the glass will stick to the mold.

515. Expansion and contraction of the kiln during firing will eventually cause the case of the kiln to loosen. To prevent this, the clamps on the jacket, lid, and bottom of the kiln should be tightened occasionally when the kiln is warm.

516. The observation holes of the kiln allow viewing of the firing chamber and pyrometric cones. They also provide an escape for water vapor and gases.

517. Excess glare from a hot firing chamber can be reduced by using dark glasses or a number five welder's lens when looking through the observation holes.

518. Kiln elements will become brittle after a few firings, so care should be taken if handling is necessary.

519. A kiln sitter is a mechanical control that will shut off your kiln when a pyrometric one reaches maturity and bends to a predetermined angle. When the kiln sitter is off, the kiln will no longer fire.

520. The elements in your kiln are designed for a long life and are capable of many firings. The life span can be shortened by contact with materials such as bits of bisque, glaze, cones, metal or kiln wash. Keep elements clean.

521. A kiln sitter is called an automatic shut-off, but it should not be left unattended. An uncontrollable accident such as greenware falling against the end of the kiln sitter tube may cause an overfiring which could damage your kiln. If this happens you should be near at hand to shut it off manually, within an hour of estimated firing time.

522. Do not place greenware and glazed ware in the same load. The gases emitted by greenware may cause discoloration of the glaze.

523. If it is necessary to mix glaze and greenware pieces when firing a load, the glazed pieces should be loaded in the lower part of the kiln with greenware above.

524. Many repairs on your kiln can be done by removing an old or damaged part and inserting a new one.

525. If large flat pieces are being fired in your kiln, the edges should be placed between the elements. This may eliminate possible cracking from uneven heating.

526. When firing greenware, it can touch other greenware as well as the kiln shelves. Kiln washed shelves are not necessary when firing only greenware.

527. Do not load red family glazes, green, yellow, or yellow-green glazes, metallic or lustre glazes in your kiln with greenware.

528. Allow a minimum of two inches of space around red glazed pieces.

529. Firing is your most important step in ceramics. All your hard work on a piece can be ruined and you kiln permanently damaged from careless loading or firing.

530. Bisque or low fire glaze firings (04-06) usually require 5 to 7 hours firing time. Porcelain and stoneware high firings take from 6 to 10 hours.

531. If the fuse or circuit breaker in your home fails after firing your kiln, it could be due to an inadequate fuse or breaker, inadequate wiring size or a defective fuse or breaker.

532. Cones come in two sizes. Small cones 1-1/8" long are used in kiln sitters and large cones 2-1/4" long are placed throughout the load, and at the level of the kiln sitter to determine temperature variations and the accuracy of the kiln sitter. The latter are called "witness" cones.

533. The shorter length and higher density of the small cone makes them stand longer than larger cones when placed on ends. However, when used in the kiln sitter, the small cones bend at the same time as large cones standing.

534. If cones are exposed to moisture during their life, they may crack and bend prematurely when fired.

535. If you have problems with cracked cones because they become damp, drying them will not correct the damage. Use another box. Always store cones in a dry place.

536. When firing allow at least one element grove between every shelf. If your kiln has a blank spacer ring, let a least two element grooves contribute to the heat of the blank space.

537. If it takes longer now for your kiln to fire, it could be caused by a defective switch or element, or may even be the wall receptacle.

538. If your kiln will not heat, the power cord may be plugged in, fuses or breakers blown, kiln sitter not activated or power cord burned.

539. If, when firing, your wall receptacle or plug heats up, check to see if there is a loose connection in the receptical.

540. If a kiln makes popping noises when firing, it is normal. This is due to the contraction of kiln parts which are enlarged from thermal expansion.

541. The top of almost every kiln is coated with a thin, high-temperature coating. This makes the lid more durable and prevents dusting of the brick particles on the pieces in the firing chamber.

542. If an element pops loose from a groove, this may be due to the loosening of the pins caused by expansion and contraction of the element during heating and cooling.

543. If the lid of your kiln becomes chipped or damaged, simply smooth the surface of the hole with sandpaper and blow or vacuum clean. A seal coat may be spread thinly over the exposed brick to seal it and prevent dusting.

544. Sometimes the bottom of kilns do become damaged due to glaze drippings. If in cleaning these drippings you've created holes in the floor of the kiln, you can mix kiln wash to a paste consistency and fill the hole allowing the paste to dry before firing.

545. If your kiln overfires, your kiln sensing rod on the kiln sitter is probably blocked or it is not in adjustment. The kiln may not be level, something has blocked the sitter or possibly the sitter is defective.

546. If your kiln sitter shuts off your kiln before maturing pieces, it may be caused by a kiln sitter out of adjustment, a blown fuse or circuit breaker, the wrong cone in the sitter, the cone becoming knocked loose during firing or an incorrectly set kiln-timer.

547. A gap between the lid and the bottom of the kiln during the firing process is caused by the distorition of the kiln from thermal expansion.

548. Every time you get ready to fire your kiln, check the inside to be sure it is clean and free of dust. Check the lid and wall brick for loose fragments which might fall on the ware. If possible, vacuum the interior to remove all dust and foreign materials from the elements.

549. Due to heat, corrosion and mechanical wear, the kiln sitter may get out of adjustment over a period of normal operation. The repeated fall of the weight of the kiln sitter may possibly force the trigger to creep. To insure consistent firing it is recommended that the adjustment of the sitter be checked about every 20 firings.

550. If the lid of your kiln does gap in front, loosen the hinge screws a half turn when the kiln is hot. This allows the lid to reposition itself thus compensating for heat expansion. After repositioning, retighten the hinge screws.

551. The danger in glass sagging is fast cooling, rather than fast firing.

552. If you have students who like to hand model or want to try it yourself, handle the firing of these pieces the same way as your normal ceramic firing.

553. Terra Cotta clay is the normal modeling clay used in ceramics and matures at cone 06 to 04. It should be fired on a slower schedule than cast ware.

554. When firing stoneware in your kiln, it is necessary to use the same precautions in loading your kiln as you would for porcelain. Stoneware is fired at cone 4 through cone 8 and at these temperatures it becomes almost vitreous.

555. Your kiln is hotter near the sides and the side of the ware next to these walls will tend to shrink more than the opposite side. This is particularly so when firing porcelain. This can be used to your advantage when firing figurines that tend to warp in the firing process. Turn the inside of the porcelain figure away from the elements and heat will help to hold it straight.

556. The length of firing time for glass sagging is less than ceramics. Place an 015 and 014 cone in your kiln in a pat of clay and fire until the 014 is halfway down, turn off the kiln and cool slowly.

557. If you use a cone mounted in a piece of clay to fire your kiln, it should be mounted at an 8 degree incline from the vertical.

558. When you are giving your kiln bottom a new coat of kiln wash, be sure to put cardboard against the sides to protect the elements.

559. Always use the proper cone. Do not try to get by with one that is close if you are out of the proper one.

560. When firing porcelain lying flat on a shelf or a box and its lid, the undersides should be protected with silica to prevent parts of the pieces from sticking to each other and to shelves.

561. If you have a piece of porcelain that comes out of the kiln without translucent quality, you may be pouring the piece too thick or be underfiring.

562. Bumps in porcelain are usually caused by wet greenware and overfired porcelain bisque.

563. Holes in lace or fabric which appear after firing can be caused by inadequate application of slip.

564. Damp greenware or mended places will cause bumps on the surface of fired ware if you do not allow a piece to dry before firing.

565. The stilted plate leaves the bottom exposed to radiation from the sidewalls.

566. When you fire lace figurines, leave the peep hole plugs out and the lid propped open until all smoke and odor are gone.

567. There is nothing mysterious or complex about a kiln and you have no reason to be afraid of it. No two kilns are exactly alike, even if they are the same brand and model.

568. Your electrical installation for your kiln will be as good as the electrician you use.

569. To get like firings every time, you must place your cone in the automatic kiln sitter in exactly the same way each time you fire your kiln.

570. You should learn to adjust and operate your kiln sitter before firing. You should recheck this periodically.

571. It is important that you do not let any ware touch the elements of the kiln. You may not only damage the elements themselves, but you are sure to damage your ware.

572. A thermocouple is the measuring unit of a pyrometer which is inserted into the firing chamber of the kiln through a hole that is drilled in one of the peep hole plugs.

573. When firing plates, position them between the elements for proper heat distribution.

574. Kiln shelves may be supported by either three or four posts. Place these posts on the floor of the kiln at the same time the floor is being loaded. Do not use a post shorter than 2-1/2".

575. When loading your kiln with porcelain glazed pieces, the process is similar to loading porcelain bisque. Lightweight ware and small pieces should be placed on the bottom of the kiln for best circulation of air and distribution of heat.

576. When firing porcelain, you do not use stilts. All glazed ware must be dryfooted. Be sure you have a good coat of porcelain kiln wash on the shelves and floor of the kiln before you load your ware.

577. If in firing porcelain, a piece of ware had to be supported in the bisque firing, it will stand alone in glaze firing. The lower temperature will prevent sagging.

578. Holes in lace or fabric which appear after firing, can be avoided by first washing fabric thoroughly before dipping into slip. Apply enough slip to the fabric so the clay will be strong enough to hold its own weight. The fabric must burn out before the clay matures, leaving only the clay shell.

579. Plateholders insure even firing of china painted plates.

580. When firing porcelain, two pieces of ware that are to be used together must be fired together. Powdered silica must be added to touch edges to prevent pieces from sticking together in firing.

581. Although an automatic kiln sitter does turn off the kiln, it is a mechanical device and cannot be considered an absolute guarantee against overfiring.

582. If you are having your home wired, make the following checks of the job before the electrician leaves. Place all switches on high-heat position and watch the elements with the kiln lid open. The elements should come up to a dull red color over a period of several minutes. If any element or any pair of elements turns bright red within 20-30 seconds, turn the kiln off and have the electrician check to be sure that the ground neutral wire of the circuit is connected to the proper terminal at the fuse box or circuit breaker box and the neutral terminal of the receptical. Failure to do this can cause damage to the elements or to the switches.

583. In purchasing kiln furniture, avoid triangular posts that are taller than 10" or square posts that are taller than 14".

584. Your kiln will give you years of service if you care for it properly. It should not be considered as a household appliance, but rather a piece of hard working machinery.

585. Most ceramic bodies have only one exact point at which they will mature properly. There is no way that you can control or guarantee the kiln being turned off at just the right point, except by using the proper cone and watching it closely to protect your ware.

586. If you get a chipped area in your kiln lid it should be repaired immediately.

587. Reds mature at a lower temperature than other colors and are fired after the other colors have been fired. Reds and yellows should not be fired side by side.

588. Colors mature at a lower temperature on ceramic pieces than on porcelain or hard china.

589. The heating elements must be at a greater temperature than the rest of the kiln in order for heat to be transferred. This causes the area around the elements to be considerably hotter and no piece should be closer than 1" to a coil.

590. Larger pieces that take all of the kiln dimensions should be placed so that the projecting edges are between coils.

591. Ceramic ware that is used together should be fired together such as a box and its lid.

592. Ceramic glaze will fire like ceramic bisque, except that it usually fires to a lower cone and less time will be required.

593. For the most economical use of posts and kiln capacity, place ware approximately the same height in each layer.

594. Be sure to fire ceramic bisque hard enough to eliminate any chance of the fired piece absorbing moisture. Moisture absorbed after the piece has been glazed will cause it to expand and crack the glazed surface, which is called crazing.

595. Stilts should be used to support the glaze ware during firing to prevent sticking to the shelves or floor.

596. Plates fired on edges may be supported at the bottom with large spur stilts which can also be used to separate adjoining plates. Tall posts can be used to separate plates from the walls.

597. A kiln will operate properly only if the circuit you use is correctly connected. If you plan to use an existing circuit, be sure that it is large enough and is not used for other purposes while the kiln is firing.

598. Overglazed ware is loaded into the kiln in the same manner as loading a glaze firing. Ware must be prevented from sticking by the use of stilts, and it must not touch other pieces of ware.

599. You should always inspect a new kiln when it arrives. Vibration and jarring in shipping sometimes causes elements in the kiln to become dislodged.

600. Never fire by time alone . . . always use a pyrometric cone.

601. You need a good assortment of shelves, posts and stilts to get maximum use from your kiln.

602. A pryometer indicates when it is time to start watching the cone in kilns without automatic kiln sitters. It is not a substitute for the cone.

603. Since cones are made from similar material to the ware being fired in a kiln and are subjected to the same heat treatment as the ware being fired, it is the most accurate indicator of proper firing time.

604. Try to place your heaviest load of ware in the layer in the kiln that has the most element grooves included.

605. Be sure that at least one element groove is between the top shelf and the top of the kiln.

606. The first layer in the kiln should be small, light pieces.

607. Do not put peep hole plugs in your kiln until the first switch is on high.

608. Keep curtains, paper walls, inflamable materials and children away from your kiln.

609. The insulating firebrick expands and contracts with each firing. The expansion and contraction is necessary for the long life of your kiln, but some hair line cracks will appear in the brick while the kiln is cold. Do not be concerned about them, as they close tightly when the bricks expand when heated.

610. Apply kiln wash to the bottom of your kiln and one side (top) of your shelves before your first glaze firing.

611. Shelves are made especially for the kiln in which they will be used and come in a variety of shapes. Half shelves increase kiln space by making it possible to fire tall pieces beside one or more layers of small pieces.

612. Kiln shelves are strong, but like other pieces of pottery and ceramics, will break if dropped and should be handled carefully

613. Peep holes in your kiln are used for

observing the firing process so that you can see when the cone bends and when it is time to turn the kiln off if you do not have an automatic shut off.

614. Peep holes have a secondary function in that they draw oxygen into the kiln, preventing reduction, and carry off smoke and water vapor.

615. If you have just purchased a new kiln, it will give longer and better service if broken-in carefully. Moisture is present in the kiln from water used in manufacturing and this must be dried out by pre-heating.

616. Check the kiln frequently during the first few firings, and note the color inside of the kiln so that you can learn to estimate the temperature with accuracy.

617. If chips should appear in the lid of your kiln, they should be repaired immediately to prevent them from becoming larger.

618. The bottom of your kiln should be covered with kiln wash at all times. If glaze drippings accumulate, they should be scraped off and a new coating of kiln wash be applied.

619. If you kiln stops heating during a firing be sure to check your fuses or circuit breakers first. Be sure you know what fuses or switches control your kiln and how to replace them.

620. A blown fuse or tripped circuit breaker is not necessarily an indication of an electrical problem in your kiln or wiring.

621. If, your kiln heats in some switch positions, but not in all, you may have a blown fuse, defective element, switch or element connection which can be corrected by replacing a fuse or resetting a breaker. Be sure to locate defective parts if necessary and replace.

622. If you think you have a problem inside the kiln during the firing cycle turn it off and allow to cool before opening.

623. If you have a hot plug or outlet, one or both may be defective and should be replaced if they are too hot to hold. Do not refire until fixed.

624. The plugs that are used in the peep holes are not put in to prevent heat loss, but to stop air from entering the kiln.

625. Stilts are small clay supports with points on the upper portion to support glazed pieces during firing.

626. It is not necessary for your peep hole plugs to fit tightly, as it is good to have some air entering the kiln at all times. Peep holes should be as small as possible to control the air flow, but large enough to see the cone clearly.

627. A pryometer is used to measure the progress of firing and determine accurately the best time to turn switches on the kiln to high, low or medium.

628. The medium heat setting on your kiln will build-up the temperature in the kiln, but as it is an uneven heating, it should be used only for equalizing the temperature in a one switch kiln. In two switch kilns, use medium for building up the temperature gradually through the middle range, but always in a sequence that will keep the bottom of the kiln hotter than the top.

629. Heat or temperature is equalized when you turn all the switches to the high setting.

630. One of the first things to consider in locating your kiln is that it should be convenient to an electrical outlet and is in a well-ventilated area.

631. When setting up your kiln, avoid placing it on rubber tiles, linoleum, or on any surface that might tend to mar if heated.

632. When locating your kiln it is best to place it on asbestos tile or a cement floor. If you need to place it on a floor that may be heat marred, lay down a few squares of asbestos for it to rest on.

633. Kiln wash is a non-hardening compound that consists of a combination of dry powder and water, and is applied by painting a fairly thick coating to one side of shelves and the floor of the kiln.

634. A pryometric cone is a small pyramid of clay and mineraloxide.

635. When the surfaces of your kiln floor or shelves which are protected by kiln wash become rough, they should be scraped off and a new coat added.

636. The same firing schedule is used for both porcelain bisque and porcelain glaze. The low heat period of your kiln can be shortened by two or three hours for glaze firing.

637. Black specks in the ware are usually caused by organic materials not completely burned out in the bisque firing. They work their way to the surface during a glaze firing.

638. Warped ware can be caused by distortion upon removal of the piece from the mold, being fired too close to the elements or firing a piece in an unnatural position.

639. Vitrify means that an item changes into glass or glassy state by heat and fusion.

640. Posts, which are made from the same material as kiln shelves, will withstand the same amount of temperature and are used to support and separate the layers of shelves being fired in the kiln. Shorter posts have greater stability.

641. The primary value of a kiln sitter is the convenience of being relieved of watching the cones and produces a uniform firing which can be consistent from one firing to the next.

642. Total firing time is controlled by the length of time the kiln is left on low. The medium heat position should be used only for balancing the heat between the top and bottom of a kiln.

643. When adding a shelf to the kiln, hold it by the edges and hold it carefully so the sidewall of the kiln will not be damaged.

644. If you fire only bisque, it is not necessary to use kiln wash on the bottom of your kiln.

645. It is important to remember that one element grove must be between every shelf with the exception of half shelves.

646. Before you turn your kiln on be sure that no two pieces are touching each other, the kiln walls, floor or shelves.

647. Stilts cannot be used to support porcelain bisque as they become embedded in the porcelain when heated to high temperatures.

648. If you break a piece while loading your kiln go ahead and repair it but do not attempt to fire before it is bone dry.

649. Glazed pieces may be prevented from sticking to the bottom of the kiln if you remove the glaze. This is called "dry footing."

650. Your kiln should be cleaned thoroughly before firing when new. This can best be done with a nozzel attachment to a vacuum cleaner or a damp cloth or sponge.

651. If your kiln fires too fast, slow it down by leaving the switches on low longer. You can speed up firing by changing the switches to a higher position sooner.

652. Never apply kiln wash to the side walls, lid, or bottom of shelves, as it will fall off during firing and ruin your glazed ware.

653. A kiln shelf is a flat slab of fired clay which has been fired to a higher temperature than will be encountered in your kiln.

654. A kiln sitter is an electrical switch which is turned on by hand and turned off by the action of a cone bending under a rod.

655. When the switch on a kiln sitter is turned off, the power to the kiln is interrupted so that no more heat can go into the kiln.

656. A pyrometer will measure temperatures in a kiln from 100 degrees F. to 2300 degrees F.

657. The low heat position of the switches on a kiln provides a means of limiting the rate of temperature increase in the early part of a firing. A fairly slow but even heating rate is important in preventing breakage.

658. After glaze firings, the stilts are removed from the ware by breaking the thin film of glaze holding them. Handling with caution, remove the sharp edges. This can be done by grinding off with a carbarundum stone, electric grinder or hand grinder.

659. China paints must not be applied heavily, as this will cause cracking or peeling when fired.

660. All china paint colors do not reach maximum color and brilliancy at the same temperature, even when they are fired on the same ware. It is important to know which colors to fire first to the higher temperatures so not to burn out the lower temperature colors.

661. Since all heat rises, the bottom of a kiln is the hardest part to heat. Because of this, as much of the bottom of the kiln should be exposed to radiation from the side walls as possible.

662. Two of the element grooves should be between the bottom of the kiln and the first shelf. The first layer in the kiln should be small, light pieces, with ample room for air circulation around their bases.

663. Placing small, low pieces on the bottom of the kiln uses your furniture more efficiently as tall pieces may be placed on the top shelf and other posts and shelves do not have to go over the tall pieces.

664. The most important item that goes into your kiln is the cone. It merits careful placement and sufficient space in planning your load.

665. When loading your kiln, leave ample room between each piece for air circulation

666. When loading your kiln, place greenware directly on the shelves or the floor of the kiln. Greenware can be stacked so it touches other greenware.

667. Fire bisque at least one cone hotter than glaze and even more if glaze can be applied easily.

668. Glazed ware and bisque ware should not be fired together unless both mature at the same cone. Even then, be sure that the glaze is loaded in the bottom of the kiln.

669. There is one basic difference between loading greenware and glaze. Glazed pieces cannot touch anything.

670. You can remove sharp points of glaze left by stilts by rubbing with a carborundum stone.

671. A kiln must be vented until all china paint oil and other organic materials have been burned out.

672. Plates with overglazes on them will fire better when supported by a plate holder or placed on edge to permit even heating.

673. Did you know that "high fired" means that the ceramic body is fired to cone 4 or higher?

674. If you would like to try sagging glass, one thing to remember is that your shelves and kiln must be level. If not, your glass will not be symmetrical.

675. Broken lines in gold can be caused by over-firing or too heavy an application.

676. Weakening of lustre colors can be caused by over-firing.

677. Did you know that "silica" or flint is a mineral which will not harden at firing temperatures and is used for separating porcelain pieces during firing?

678. Poor color in colored glazes can be caused by over-firing. This is especially true of red glazes which are usually fired at a lower temperature.

679. The average cast piece may be fired on a fast firing schedule. Slow firing of heavy pieces reduces danger of breakage and many people feel that slow firing produces better ware.

680. Remember! Ceramic greenware must be bone dry before placing in a kiln. Wet greenware will crack in firing.

681. If you use a cone holder in firing, you can make one very easily by taking a teaspoon of slip and pouring it on a plaster bat or mold. Stick a cone in it and you have a perfect cone holder.

682. Leave peep hole plugs out of your kiln until it is turned on high.

683. Porcelain bisque should always be fired slowly.

684. To avoid getting a big pile up of glaze on stilts, try coating them with kiln wash.

685. A slow firing is always preferable to a fast firing.

686. The heavier a kiln is loaded the longer the firing cycle.

687. If you use pieces of mica under touching parts of dryfooted articles, you can keep the glaze from dripping onto shelves.

688. You should get into the habit of checking your pieces when removing from the kiln and before you remove stilts, in case they need refiring.

689. If you are going to refire a piece of glazed ware, but are having difficulty making the stilts stick to the bottom, try glue. The glue will not effect the piece and fire off.

690. If the kiln floor becomes rough and the shelves are difficult to keep level or steady, try putting small wads of clay under each post until it rests solid.

691. If some of your lids will not fit after you add glaze and fire, you are not leaving enough room for the coats of glaze.

692. If you find that your glazes do not seem to stick after firing, you may have overfired your bisque originally.

693. Pieces that are heavily glazed should be kept further apart during firing to avoid glaze running from one piece to another.

694. Your underglazes may run if you overfire but you may also find that you are applying glazes too heavily and they are "pulling" your underglaze from the surface.

695. You cannot use a clock to time your firing instead of a cone. Many kilns are equipped with limit timers that will shut them off to prevent over-firing but time does not control accurate firing.

696. If you do not want the inside of your kiln lid to turn black during a gold or lustre firing, tape a piece of asbestos paper on the underside of the lid. Lap the paper over the outside edges and tape to the top of the lid. The temperature is not hot enough to effect the masking tape on top and the paper will protect the lid.

697. If you plan to refire a glazed piece and need to stilt it, coat the bottom with a light coat of clear glaze. This will give the bottom a texture and keep it from slipping off stilts.

698. Kiln wash is normally used to protect the bottom of a kiln and one side of shelves from glaze drippings. If you prefer, however, you can use asbestos paper. After paper becomes brittle or spotted, you can change to a new piece.

699. When firing porcelain cups, do not place one inside of the other. It is possible to place two cups on top of each other during firing if the rims match up and each rim has been coated with flint.

700. A bisque tile can serve the same purpose as a shelf when firing jewelry or other light pieces.

701. Hand modeled pieces should be fired alone and on a slow firing schedule.

702. If you discover bubbles in your glaze after firing, you may be firing too rapidly. Slow down your firing cycle. Gases and air bubbles must be allowed to escape during the firing process by "soaking" the glaze with a longer firing.

703. You must always vent your kiln lid (prop it open) during the firing of gold, lustres and decals. You must allow the gases o escape during the firing process.

704. Don't throw away any kiln shelves that you accidently break. They will come in handy during special firings of pieces when you know that glaze might run. You may also use them only part way across your kiln, allowing a large or tall piece to be placed on a lower shelf up past your broken shelf.

705. If you should happen to get broken, wiggly lines on your piece after a gold firing you may be over-firing.

706. Did you know that a "Vertical Setter" was a rack to hold plates during china firing?

707. It is difficult to predict when your kiln will shut off but you can narrow the time down to an approximate hour. The number of pieces you are firing will vary this a great deal.

708. The amount of kiln furniture you use in loading a kiln will effect the firing time too.

709. Did you know that "pre-firing" is a test firing of a kiln to check the function of a kiln when new?

710. Did you know that "tile setters" are racks used to fire tiles to keep them from warping during firing?

711. There is a reason for that odor when firing your golds or other lustres. They are suspended in resins and oils so you can apply them properly. During the firing process, these must be burned out so you will get that fine finish.

712. If you do not vent your kiln properly when firing, your pieces will have a cloudy appearance and often an impaired finish.

713. Did you know that "bars" are not places where you drink? They are a variety of stilts in the shape of a bar which can vary in length and have sharp nichrome wire points protruding.

714. Don't remove fired pieces from your kiln until they have cooled enough to handle comfortably. Removing pieces too soon will cause cracks in ware and singed fingers.

715. Firing wet glazes may cause pinholes, cracking or bubbling. If this should happen, try refiring the piece.

716. Keep your kiln away from your home living area. Wherever you locate it, it should be well-ventilated so the fumes that are emitted will not bother other members of the family.

717. It is important to keep the outside of kiln clean too. The elimination of dust is of particular importance as it can settle on ware and cause defects.

718. If you have a piece that has crazed after firing, you can often correct this by refiring your piece a cone or two hotter than the original firing.

719. A "flux" is composed of lead, lime or other materials that are combined with ceramic clays to reduce the speed and maturing temperature during firing.

720. If you have a glaze that is supposed to have a texture after firing, and it does not, you may not be applying enough of the glaze or are over-firing.

721. In the firing process, "volatilization" means the action produced within a firing where some materials are changed from a solid to a gaseous state, such as water turning to steam.

722. A "limit timer" is the term used for the timing device that may be installed on a kiln to shut off the power at a predetermined and set time.

723. Common in pottery is the term "oxidation," which is the method of firing a kiln in a manner that mixes oxygen with the fuel to produce a clean flame with no soot or smoke and complete combustion. The atmosphere within the kiln contains sufficient oxygen to allow the elements in the clay and glaze to be completely oxidized. This method is primarily attempted using gas kilns.

724. Pinholes in glaze can be caused by underfired bisque, applying glaze on greenware or firing too rapidly. Sometimes these holes are in the greenware and should be rubbed out before firing. If pinholes appear in the glaze, fill holes with glaze and refire.

725. A reduction firing is an incomplete burning where smoke and soot (the excess carbon) rob the clay body and glazes of part of their oxygen, thus changing their color and texture. This is primarily a firing technique in pottery.

726. Gray areas in red glazes are caused by not enough glaze. Reds must always be applied on bisque, never greenware.

727. If the floor of your kiln has some rough spots caused from chipping off glaze drippings you can patch it with a special cement. You may also want to place an extra shelf in the bottom for protection.

728. Did you know that "droppings" are drips of glazes from pieces during the firing process?

729. When loading your kiln, do not pack it too full. It is a bad habit to stack things inside of each other, on top or in any combination to save space. Too much of this and the stress caused may result in cracked bisque.

730. If your kiln is not equipped with an automatic shut off and you do not desire to have one, place your cones directly in front of the peep hole. The cones can be inserted in a pat of clay.

731. The kiln should always be started with your switches on low regardless of the type of firing. This reduces shock and dispels moisture from ware slowly.

732. You can fire glass and ceramics at the same time as long as you use the proper temperatures for each item.

733. You can protect the bottom of your kiln by placing a full shelf there and coating it with kiln wash.

734. Did you know that "nichrome wire" is what kiln elements and stilts are made with? This is a special combination of Nichol and Chromium that will withstand the high temperatures of a kiln.

735. Avoid crowding glaze pieces, as some have the tendency to "flash" or "spit" during firing and may leave a spot of unwanted color on another of your pieces.

736. Did you know that "Blowing" means that a piece has exploded during the firing process?

737. Do not open a kiln in the middle of a firing for any reason. Let it cool gradually and you will not ruin any ware.

738. Porcelain becomes non-pourous when fired, so it must be treated as you would a glazed piece.

739. Be sure your hands are clean when loading your kiln. Oils or dirt from hands may mix with colors effecting them unwantedly.

740. If you hear something fall in your kiln while firing or if you think it is working abnormally, turn it off immediately. Wait until the kiln has cooled to the touch and open and inspect.

741. The red family of glazes is easily contaminated and requires more venting and a faster firing schedule.

742. Some manufacturers have special requirements for firing the glazes they make. Be sure to check the bottles of each color for the proper cone.

743. You can fire overglazes directly on porcelain bisque but you may have to use a hotter cone. These overglazes can be applied directly and fired in the 017-015 range.

744. When installing wiring for hooking up your kiln, be sure that the proper gauge wire is being used to carry the load. If the proper wire is not used your breaker switch or fuse will go when the kiln heats up to maximum temperatures.

745. If you have problems with your kiln, be sure to go back to the place you bought it. Normally they are happy to help you.

746. A kiln will not over-fire when you have all the switches on low because it does not attain enough heat inside. It reaches about 100 degrees.

747. A rule of thumb for removing pieces from the kiln is that you should be able to touch and handle them comfortably with your bare hands. If you cannot, they are too hot.

748. The thing to remember when firing glass is that it must be cooled quickly to keep pieces from warping or melting. Even if you do cool the pieces properly, it may be necessary to have supports for a particular glass piece to keep its proper shape.

749. Supports for glass firing may be made from fire brick cut to the proper shape or you can purchase a mold for that purpose.

750. If you fire your over-glazes and china paints too high the colors will fade.

751. If when firing a new kiln, you hear a humming noise, it is normal. This usually happens and will only last for a few firings.

752. The first few firings of a new kiln should not be glazed piece. It may take a couple of firings to get all the moisture and vapors out of the kiln from the manufacturing process.

753. Never fire a kiln in an enclosed area such as a closet.

754. Your floor may not be level but a kiln must be for proper firing. If necessary you can add shims under the legs of the stand to make it balance properly.

755. If you must move your kiln be sure to handle it by the outside which is protected with stainless steel. Fire brick is soft and can be damaged easily.

756. If you are about to plug in your kiln either for the first time or after moving it, be sure that all switchs are off before doing so.

757. Did you know that "kanthal" type elements are made of a combination of iron, chromium and aluminum?

758. The bottoms of most kilns are reversible and may be turned over if one side gets too damaged.

759. Most kilns come with a wedge cut from fire brick for propping open the kiln lid in the initial stages of firing. It may also be purchased separately.

760. Most kilns come with a locking brace to hold the lid open. Be sure that it is locked in position before leaving it unattended. The lid can fall and break or it can fall on your hand . . . that smarts!

761. The jackets on most kilns are made of stainless steel and should be kept clean. You can polish them with normal stainless steel cleaner.

762. The jacket on your kiln becomes quite warm during firing and is too hot to touch. It helps to hold and reflect heat back into the kiln.

763. Stainless steel will discolor from repeated firings, but can be cleaned.

764. Always read your instruction manual as provided by the manufacturer of your kiln. Many kilns are similar but all have their own characteristics.

765. All kilns come with some kind of guarantee. Be sure to fill out the warranty card so if you do have any problems you are covered.

766. If you use cones for firing that need to be mounted in a pat of clay and placed in front of a peep hole you might find a cone holder designed for that purpose easier to use.

767. If you look in your kiln through a peep hole, pieces that are near the same temperature will be the same color. Brighter objects are hotter than darker objects.

768. If your kiln is equipped with an automatic shut off you should coat the top of the cone support and the bottom of the sensing rod with kiln wash to prevent sticking of cones.

769. It is possible to vary the temperature at which your automatic shut-off works by the position of the cone. Positioning the thinner part of a pyramid shaped cone under the sensing rod will make it shut off sooner while the thicker part makes it fire longer.

770. If you use a test cone when firing, it should be placed about three inches behind a peep hole so you can see it easily.

771. Spacing is important when firing lustres to prevent contamination.

772. If you have craters in your glaze, they can be saved by putting glaze in the craters and refiring to one cone hotter.

773. Glaze will creep in the firing if the bisque was oily or greasy, dirty or dusty. You can salvage the piece by reglazing and refiring.

774. Did you know that "pigtail" was the doubled and twisted end of a heating element?

775. Kilns with less than three inch sidewalls may require one cone hotter temperatures than those with thicker walls to do the same job.

776. Purple spots in gold are usually due to a thin application of gold or too much thinner.

777. "Venting" means allowing air to come into the kiln and the gases to escape.

778. If you have over-fired glass, the edges will have needle points and the finish will be dull.

779. If you want to retain the shape of a glass piece that has been painted, you should not fire it above 022 as the glass will soften and distort above this temperature.

780. Check all pieces after removing from the kiln. Defects can occur and you should note them when you take them out of the kiln and avoid the same mistake in future firings.

781. Remember, that you do not go away and leave your kiln firing unattended.

782. When painting glass such as bottles, use the same loading and firing procedure as you would for overglaze.

783. A standard electric kiln normally requires 220-240 single phase voltage to work properly. It is possible to fire your kiln on a 208 volt source, but firing times may be slower. If your kiln should be wired for 208 volts you cannot use it on a 240 volt source.

784. It is a good idea to keep a record of your firing times. Some types of pieces or loads will fire faster or slower than others. If you have a record, you can get results each time by knowing ahead of time how to fire a load.

785. When firing china paints, you should vent your kiln on low and medium heat settings and close the lid when turning to high.

786. The coils in your elements should not be so close together that they touch each other.

General Tips and Hints

787. Marbleizing liquid is a water-based product and the brush should be cleaned in soap and water.

788. If you experience difficulty in seeing what areas of your bisque you have or have not covered with white opaque stain, you can dampen your piece lightly with a sponge and those areas that you have missed will show up and through, usually a little on the yellowish side.

789. Stoneware is a mixture of clays used in a manner similar to how they are found in nature, without the addition of stabilizing ingredients.

790. You can do something with old broken molds. First try matching two broken halves for something new or use them as open pour molds. The piece from the open pour possibly could be attached to something else.

791. You should always fill the handles of cups with pouring. If they do not fill by letting excess slip settling into them, paint them full with a brush.

792. In cleaning bone-dry greenware, you may find nylon tulle easier to use since it is finer.

793. You can apply raised designs to wet greenware by using a brush syringe or eyedropper filled with slip.

794. If you have a problem with pinholes appearing in your glaze, try sponging it on rather than using a brush.

795. You can protect an airbrushed piece that smears easily by spraying on a light coating of glue before firing. You can then handle piece for placement in kiln without worry.

796. Attractive edges on plates or special designs on vases are possible by sponging color through plastic or other dollies.

797. You should stir all colors well before applying except for a few. In setting on the shelf, many colors settle and stirring will help to mix them again.

798. A pipe cleaner can be a handy clean-up tool for those really small areas on greenware.

799. A coating of clear spray will help seal metallic colors and make them easier to antique.

800. You can use clear spray fixative for sealing those pieces you have decorated with gold leaf.

801. If you have trouble making fine lines in features, try the end of your lace tool. Tip it in color and use it like a paint brush or fountain pen.

802. You can create an interesting finish by mixing a cup of slip with a teaspoon of vinegar and painting it on a greenware piece.

803. There are lots of plastic squeeze bottles on the market today and they can be used in many ways for decorating ceramics. Slip trailing is just one idea.

804. It is possible to thicken china paints with castor oil.

805. Soft bisque is greenware fired to cone 018. You should keep a couple of "pencil" shaped pieces of this soft bisque around to fill cracks or holes in your bisque pieces before decorating.

806. If you do not have a turntable, you can position your piece on a paper plate and place it on a glazed surface or even a slick table top. Turn it as you need to and then remove it when done.

807. If you need an emergency airbrush, try using a spray bottle, insect sprayer or even your vacuum cleaner.

808. You can make an unusual background for Christmas decorations by dipping a pine or spruce bow in slip. Fire it on a tile and spray-glaze it.

809. If you get tired of shaking and mixing those jars of paint, try adding a few "split shot" sinkers to each jar.

810. When you have trouble with the nozzles of spray cans plugging, try soaking them in fingernail polish remover.

811. Thin eyelashes on figurines are hard to make. If you have trouble putting them on with a brush, go ahead and try; then go back over them with your lace tool, scratching away paint to make thin ones.

812. If you do not have a supply of those plastic peanuts to use as packing material for shipping ceramic pieces, a batch of popcorn will work.

813. Old toothbrushes can be used for decorating ceramics. The bristles are stiff and can be used as a spatter brush.

814. If you are working on greenware plates and have trouble handling them without breakage, try carrying them around in paper plates.

815. A regular rubber eraser will remove unfired one-stroke from bisque in most cases.

816. Always wipe off rims of paint jars before storing. Store jars upside down. This will make opening and mixing easier.

817. An old eyedropper can be used for a variety of techniques.

818. Some colors have shorter shelf lives than others. They may become like a gel if too old. You can salvage these by stirring or even running them through your blender. Add a drop of water at a time to get the proper consistency.

819. A comb can become a texturing tool when scraped on a piece of greenware.

820. If you need to weight down a bookend or lamp, you may find it easier to use a combination of sand and plaster of paris. Plaster alone may crack the piece and sand can ooze out.

821. A piece of terry cloth will help close holes faster than a sponge on greenware.

822. If your pieces such as vases, cups, etc., require that you glaze the bottoms, let them stand to dry on stilts. This will allow the air to reach them easily and will prevent a drip line.

823. Some odd size pieces of sheet rock (plasterboard) will come in handy to store wet greenware. It is made of plaster and heavy paper and will absorb water from greenware and help to keep pieces from warping.

824. If you have difficulty cleaning between the fine fingers of your figurines because they are so tiny, try using an emery board.

825. The next time you have an appointment with the dentist, be sure to ask him to give you a few of his worn out dental tools. They come in real handy for cleaning and even can be used for design work.

826. Those stir sticks you get with a high-ball the next time you are out on the town should be saved as they make excellent stir sticks for mixing glazes and stains.

827. If you want to create an unusual design on a piece, use one of those plastic doilies as a stencil. Simply lay one on a piece and sponge color through the holes. through the holes.

828. If you need to divide a plate or pot into three equal parts, you can use the top part of a lamp shade frame. The ring in the center can be used as a guide.

829. Having difficulty in keeping track of the number of coats of glaze you have applied to a piece? Get yourself a stitch counter at a yarn store and mount it in front of you to use it. You just have to remember to change it with each coat.

830. The next time you receive a gift or buy something new, be sure to save those pieces of styrofoam that are usually packed in the boxes. These pieces of styrofoam can also be used to hold those small bottles of lustre to prevent them from tipping over when working on a project.

831. You know how you get those spray cans of household items with the bead inside to help mix them when you shake the can? You can do the same thing by adding a marble to a jar of color before you mix it and it will help you complete the job.

832. Do you need to cut a hole in a piece of greenware? While it is still wet, use a washer or even the metal lid from any can as a pattern. The cutout will be perfectly round.

833. When working on figurines or animals be sure to include the highlights in the eyes. This is a small reflection of light in the iris, to the side of the pupil. It can be added with the tip of a sgrafitto tool, pin or lace tool for a tiny dab of white. Do not allow the white eyeball to show above the iris as this gives a fixed staring expression to the face.

834. When using one-strokes for outlining do not thin them too much as y ou want as concentrated a color as possible for making lines.

835. To help remove the lid from a jar, place it on the floor and roll the top of the jar with the ball of the foot back and forth several times.

836. While you are cleaning a number of pieces, be sure to save the greenware bits that you cleaned off. When you finish, catch all the scrapings in a bisque cup and fire. This residue can be used as a fine grog that can be used to fill in cracks in bisque.

837. Be sure your hands are always clean while working on greenware. Any kind of hand cream may cause stains or hard spots on fired ware.

838. When mending greenware, be sure both sides of the crack or break are damp before using mender or slip to repair. This will help your mending agent adhere much better and form a permanent seal.

839. You always need something soft to pack greenware pieces in and those plastic bags you get from the cleaners make excellent packing material when wadded up.

840. Fingernail polish can be used to add a bit of color to those areas on a finished figurine that you may have missed. Remember, however, that this type of polish has a high sheen so be sure that is what you want before you use it.

841. Having a problem breaking greenware when you are cleaning? You can prevent this by creating "soft bisque". This is done by firing your greenware pieces to cone 018 before you start to clean. The bisque will still be soft enough to clean, yet hard enough to allow you to handle without easily being broken.

842. If you are filling cracks in greenware with slip, be sure to work the slip into the cracks as deeply as possible to form a solid bond. You may find using a stiff brush will help, using a back and forth movement of the bristles.

843. Did you know that milk will help to seal bisque? If you have a vase that has been properly glazed but still leaks a bit when water stands in it a long time, let some milk stand in it for a couple of days. It will seal the pores and prevent leaking.

844. You should keep a piece of old carpet (not shag) handy for removing the glaze from the bottom of pieces you may want to dryfoot. It acts somewhat like sandpaper but not as abrasive.

845. Do not over-sponge your piece in the cleaning process. It is possible to make a piece too smooth, closing the pores, and preventing the piece from taking color later after it has been fired.

846. The inside of salt and pepper shakers should be glazed too. If you have trouble getting the glaze inside, use a squeeze bottle and force it in. You may also thin glaze with water to help with the job of pouring it in. Be sure to use a toothpick or tool to clear holes in top.

847. While we're talking about salt and pepper shakers, here's something to try too. It is often difficult to keep the holes in the top from filling in with glaze during the firing. Next time insert short pieces of toothpick in each hole and put them in the kiln that way. The wooden toothpick will burn out during the firing but will help to keep holes clear of glaze.

848. Decorating the yard with ceramic pieces is always a lot of fun, but many forget to prepare the inside of pieces. Be sure to glaze the inside of all your pieces as well as staining outside. This will help to protect the piece from moisture and make the decoration on the outside last a lot longer. If you do not protect the inside, moisture can get into the bisque and push the decoration off the outside, usually in the form of chipping.

849. You may often need a pliable and damp piece of clay to work with, but when you go to find one, it may be dried out. To help keep this clay moist, you can wrap it in damp cloths and store in a sealed can or jar, oil cloth or, probably best of all, a plastic bag.

850. Any type of cotton or cloth will burn out during the firing process. For a different effect, you can try soaking cloth or cotton in slip and adding it to your piece for decoration. During the firing process it will fire out leaving just the thin layer of clay that it originally absorbed. Most people think that this only applies to porcelain, but it can be used with ceramic slip as well.

851. Want to make some extra money? Talk to a florist in your area and see if you can supply him with pots for his plants or flowers. He has to buy them somewhere and it might as well be from you.

852. Use your imagination! Almost every household item or kitchen gadget you have will create a different texture when used on greenware. You may try dipping the various tools in slip as well to create designs.

853. If you like to work on pieces of clay that require rolling to form thick sheets for cutting out flower petals and leaves, you may find that the clay sticks to your roller. Next time, try putting a piece of plastic between the clay and your roller to prevent this from happening.

854. If you work with ceramics very long and like to pour molds, at some time you will spill slip on the floor. Wiping up the mess is a difficult task. One method of cleaning is to throw a handful of shredded paper on the spill. The paper will absorb the slip and when dry you can remove the spill. You might also use a large mold and place it right in the middle of the spill. Let the capillary action of the plaster work by absorbing the moisture from the slip and the clay will stick right to your mold when you pick it up.

855. If you know a builder or pass by a building project, see if you can get a few pieces of old ceiling tile. They make excellent caddies for carrying greenware, since they will be flat, are very absorbant and will collect moisture during the drying process.

856. Although there are hundreds of different tools available for the ceramist, only a basic assortment is required for the beginning ceramist.

857. A lace tool is designed to help you in the application of slip-soaked lace to greenware, but can be used for many other things.

858. All brushes are made of four parts. The tip, reservoir, ferrule and handle.

859. The tip and reservoir are probably the most important parts of any brush.

860. A basic assortment of beginning brushes will include a glaze, stain, translucent stain, feature and liner.

861. The first step in doing ceramics is the most important and that is the cleaning of greenware.

862. It is true that greenware is fragile, but it is nothing to be afraid of when cleaning.

863. When holding a piece of greenware, do it firm enough to hold it securely, but not hard enough to crack it.

864. The primary function of cleaning a piece of greenware is to remove the seam line caused by molds in the casting process.

865. The best tool to use in the beginning step of cleaning greenware is one designed for that purpose with a sharp pointed blade.

866. You will find, when starting to clean greenware, that wetting seam lines with a damp sponge will make the process easier.

867. To dampen greenware, you can use a sponge or any old plunger-type spray bottle. Remember to dampen, not drown.

868. Do not try to remove the seam line from a piece of greenware all in one pass. It is best to go over the line several times until the line is flush with the rest of your piece.

869. After the bulk of seam lines have been removed with a tool, the next step is to sand the lines with a sander sponge.

870. The final step in cleaning is to sponge your piece lightly with a damp sponge. This will guarantee smooth greenware and remove excess dust.

871. The only exception to the sponging technique in cleaning greenware is when you plan an antique wash on the finished bisque. The antiquing color may concentrate in sponge marks.

872. If, after cleaning, you see detailed areas that are not clear from either a bad casting or from your cleaning, they should be scribed or carved back into the greenware.

873. Remember that the bottom is a part of your piece too! The same care should be used in cleaning this area of greenware.

874. Be sure to test how well your piece of greenware sets on its base. By cleaning the bottom effectively, your finished piece will not wobble.

875. A piece of sandpaper attached to a table top is an effective aid in leveling the bottoms of greenware pieces.

876. After you have completed cleaning a piece of greenware, set it aside for a couple of hours and then go back and inspect it for anything you may have missed.

877. No matter how well the decoration appears on a finished figurine, poorly painted features will ruin the effect.

878. It is important to understand the composition of the eye when painting features.

879. Producing good eyes is greatly enhanced when you know how to handle your brushes comfortably.

880. Colors used for features are most commonly black or dark brown, plus the color of the eye itself.

881. Black and dark brown are fine for lashes and eyebrows but I don't ever recall seeing a blond with black eyebrows and your figurines should not be painted with them either.

882. Except on the morning after the night before, everyone's eyeball is white.

883. When painting the eyeball, be sure to stay within the boundary of the eyelids that are cast in a piece.

884. Iris portions of eyes are painted over a white eyeball so be sure the white is dry before applying.

885. Remember that we rarely see the entire iris part of our own eyes or anyone else's and you should not on a figurine.

886. A painted iris is a circle of color surrounded by a slightly darker circle of the same color.

887. Part of the iris is covered by the eye lid, usually a part of your original cast piece, therefore, you should consider that you are painting "U's" rather than circles.

888. Before adding an iris to your eyes, decide which way the figurine will be looking and paint the iris slightly left or right in that direction in both eyes.

889. The pupil in an eye is always solid black.

890. Your eye is not complete without adding a highlight to the iris. This gives a twinkle to the eye and the impression of looking in a certain direction as well.

891. Most brush-on sealers are water soluable and brushes may be cleaned effectively with water. Be sure to check label.

892. Pieces that you plan to use for food should be glazed only with "lead safe" glazes.

893. Lead safe glazes are those that are formulated to meet federal minimum standards for the amount of lead contained in the formulas.

894. You cannot tell by look at a jar of glaze what color it will look like after being fired.

895. The firing process matures the components of a glaze to give you the end color.

896. An overglaze marbleizer is a special effect product that is used with other metallic and lustre overglazes. It is applied over other products and when fired produces a star burst, spider web effect.

897. You cannot apply marbleizer to an overglazed piece until the other overglazes are completely dry.

898. All overglazes should be allowed to dry for at least 24 hours before firing.

899. Decals we use in hobby ceramics are specially formulated for that purpose. You cannot use five and dime decals to achieve the same results.

900. Technically, ceramic decals employ the use of china paints which are printed in decorative designs on special paper.

901. Many highbrow ceramists look down on decals as the easy way out for decorating ceramic pieces but don't pay any attention to them.

902. Of all the overglaze products, decals are the only one that employ water in your method of application.

903. When applying decals, it is important that all the air bubbles are removed from under the decal before it is allowed to dry. If not, a hole will result in that area during firing.

904. Be sure not to wet decals too much as they must maintain enough adhesive for a solid bond with your piece after being soaked and transferred to your piece.

905. If you leave your decal in water too long, too much glue will be removed and it will not fire properly.

906. When using decals, you may find that only parts of a decal design are required. You can easily cut them apart with a pair of scissors.

907. To avoid burn spots on your designs, you must be sure that your decal is completely dry before firing.

908. Let your decals dry at least 24 hours before firing.

909. It is imperative that the highlight painted in the eye be in the same position in both eyes. If not, your figurine will be cross-eyed.

910. Did you know that "hydrostone" is an extremely hard plaster for making master blocks and cases in master mold making?

911. Grog is fired clay which has been crushed and screened. It is used with slip or modeling clay to achieve textured effects and will reduce warping and cracking in hand modeled ware.

912. A "pipe" is the metal rod that runs through the center of lamps through which the cord passes and it is threaded on each end.

913. Spray cans of stain sealer should be held approximately 10-12" away from a piece when applying. Several light coats are much better than one heavy one.

914. To avoid runs when using a spray sealer, be sure to keep the can moving and not too close to the subject.

915. Before applying any sealer, be sure that the piece to be coated is free of any foreign debris, as it will become a part of your finished piece if allowed to remain.

916. You can apply as many coats of sealer to stains as you wish, but you must be sure that each coat is dry before adding another.

917. The most difficult aspect in using spray fixatives are the clogs that dry in spray mechanisms.

918. To help eliminate clogs in spray cans, turn the can upside down when finished with a project and push the plunger until only gas is emitted. Wipe off any excess around valve.

919. You can remove the valve from the top of a spray can for cleaning. A thin wire will clean out the hole.

920. Antiquing solvent is marketed under a variety of names, but it usually contains mineral spirits and has no odor.

921. To effectively use greenware mender, it is best to dampen both sides of a break with water and then apply a liberal amount of the mender to both sides of the break. It will form a bond in a few seconds.

922. Porcelain is composed of a blend of kaolins, china clays, ball clays and feldspars.

923. Ceramic slip (clay) goes through the stages of wet, leather-hard and dry.

924. To make clay for add-ons, all you have to do is select a flat mold or plaster bat and pour the slip on the flat surface.

925. To make an add-on, work the wet clay in your hands like bread dough, folding from time to time to eliminate air bubbles.

926. A few drops of glycerine or warm water will slow the drying time of a piece of clay you are working with your hands to form an add-on.

927. To attach an add-on to a piece of greenware, use liquid clay or slip. It is best to dampen the greenware surface before applying the add-on.

928. Be sure to apply your add-on solidly to the greenware. Any air pockets left under your add-on will make for an explosion in the kiln later.

929. When creating a new color by mixing several together, it is not a good idea to mix brands.

930. You cannot create the primary colors of red, blue and yellow through mixing.

931. In theory, you should be able to make every color on the spectrum through mixing of the primary colors red, blue and yellow.

932. To change any color to a lighter tone, simply add white to it.

933. A light color can be made darker by adding a darker color in the same tone.

934. To create completely new colors, use your primaries. Red and blue make purple. Red and yellow make orange. Yellow and blue make green. Different proportions of each will determine the hue.

935. No matter how good you become at mixing colors, it is still experimenting, and you should try the color on a piece of paper or sample chip of bisque to be sure it is what you want.

936. When cleaning a piece that you plan on making into a clock, be sure you remember to put a hole in the face for the stem of the clock-works to pass through.

937. To drill a hole in greenware, you should take care. Begin by keeping the spot for the hole as damp as possible. Start the drilling with firm but not hard pressure. Redampen the area as necessary to make the drilling easier.

938. The size of holes you drill in greenware is important. You must remember that greenware shrinks when fired. A hole should be about 10-20% larger than needed to allow for shrinkage.

939. If you have applied woodtone glaze and it comes out of the kiln with no wood grain effects, you have not brushed out the specks in the glaze enough.

940. If you are using opaque stains and they will not penetrate the bisque, you may have fired it incorrectly and it is too hard. This can also happen in spots where you might have touched greenware with greasy hands.

941. To trace a design onto a ceramic piece you can use clay carbon paper and then retrace lines onto ceramic pieces. Or trace the design you want onto onion skin and trace over the lines again with a piece of carbon paper between pattern and piece.

942. If you traced your original pattern onto your transferring paper with pencil, it is a good idea to use a different colored pencil or pen to do the second transfer so you know where you are.

943. There are several methods for putting backgrounds on a ceramic piece, including a brush, but you may find that using a sponge to add color is easier.

944. To emphasize the design, a pale color is usually a good choice for the background.

945. To tie your piece all together, you should plan your background color in advance so it uses some shade of the color in your design. Contrasting color is best.

946. The yellow colors and rose shades are considered warm colors.

947. Depth and perspective can be added to a design by using contrasting colors.

948. A monochrome is a decorating technique of a pattern painted in several tones of the same color.

949. Try to keep your designs as simple as possible. The more detailed the harder they are to paint and the more confusing to the eye.

950. You will like your finished piece better if the pattern only covers about 1/3-1/2 of your piece.

951. Never paint on flowers, etc., in even numbers. The effect of your design will be much better if you rely on odd numbers of objects in your pattern.

952. An attractive design can employ the use of two different flowers, but when you exceed that it will not only look cluttered but may be difficult to paint.

953. The darkest part of your painting of a design should be toward the base of your piece.

954. It is possible to use fine greenware dust from cleaning or clay to fill cracks or chips in ceramic greenware. Mix with water and apply.

955. One of the problems that most students have is loading too much color on a brush.

956. If you have problems with the bristles splitting during a stroke you are probably using too dry a brush. Keep it damp during application.

957. Your square brushes may go into a point while painting. This can be prevented by always stroking both sides of the brush flatly against your palette before attempting each stroke.

958. You do not have to have too many brushes. It is easy to buy them but may cause confusion as to which to use for each job.

959. Moths like brush bristles too! If you are going to store your brushes for a long time, a moth ball in the container will prevent this.

960. Newspaper makes an excellent paper for practicing brush strokes.

961. You should hold a brush like you would a dart, not a pencil.

962. If when thinning colors, you went too far, you may find a round dot of color instead of a point at the end of a stroke.

963. If you have not thinned color enough you will find that the bristles of your brush will split toward the end of your stroke.

964. A fundamental brush stroke is made with one movement of the brush.

965. Most dry brushing techniques are done with a square shader.

966. When making a reproduction doll, be sure to fire the head, arms, legs, etc., all at the same time.

967. If you want to make a reproduction doll, it is best to do a little research on it beforehand so you know a little about it and how it should look when finished.

968. When pouring dolls, use flesh colored porcelain slip as this will save you time in painting later.

969. If you are planning to add artificial eyes to your reproduction dolls, the eyes should be cut out of wet greenware.

970. When cutting out eye areas of a doll, be sure to taper the cut around the cast eye area. This will allow you to fit the eyes into their natural position later.

971. Always mark your pieces with your name and the date that you completed a project. Looking back, you will be surprised at your progress.

972. Be sure your china pieces are always clean before starting to add china color. Color seems to collect around bits of dirt and dust.

973. "Pate" is the term used that denotes covering the hole in the top of reproduction doll heads.

974. If something that you are doing in ceramics is taking you a long time each time you do it, try finding a tool to make the job easier.

975. A commercially marketed product called "Gold Off" can be used to remove china paint.

976. Stoneware slip has a tendency to settle when sitting so be sure to stir well before pouring.

977. If stoneware slip is too thick, you can thin it with a solution of 10% sodium silicate and 90% distilled water.

978. Stoneware is cast just like ceramics in molds. It takes approximately 6-8 minutes for it to set up to the desired thickness of about ¼".

979. It is possible to double cast stoneware.

980. Goldina brushes are large, round brushes composed of soft hairs.

981. When using a sgrafitto tool, you can vary the width of the line by the pressure you exert and different lines can be made by holding the tool at different angles.

982. The natural sponges that we use in ceramics are taken from the sea floor, then cleaned, bleached and dried, and sold by size, shape and quality.

983. A silk sponge has a hair-like surface with a large hole in the middle and is the finest grade of sponge.

984. To practice brush strokes, get a piece of acetate (clear plastic). Most paints will adhere to the surface and it can be washed to be used again.

985. The base color in a project is the lightest, or first, color on your brush when stroking to show multiple colors, or when shading with more than one color for contrast.

986. Did you know that another name for a stencil is "frisket"?

987. "Impasto" is a decorating technique of applying colors heavily with a palette knife or brush causing a pattern to stand out in relief.

988. When your teacher tells you to "lay in" color it means to block in an area solid with color.

989. Clay lifting is the technique of lifting up the surface of greenware to create texture or a specific design.

990. If the clay cracks when clay lifting, it may be too dry.

991. If you plan to do a clay lifting technique, your greenware should be cast heavier than normal.

992. You may use translucent stains to antique pieces finished in gold leaf.

993. Did you know that diamond dust is actually fine chips of glass that are used in decorating to simulate snow or a sparkling effect?

994. Never use a china wax pencil on porcelain as it will not fire out.

995. If you use graphite paper to transfer a design to porcelain, it can be removed with turpentine.

996. Complementary colors are any two colors that are directly opposite each other on the color wheel.

997. Never let turpentine come in contact with liquid bright gold as it will turn it purple.

998. It is possible to remove a spot of purple on a gold fired piece with rust remover.

999. Pink china paint colors will appear brown if they have been under-fired.

1000. Take all the class instruction that you can to better understand your favorite hobby, ceramics. The more knowledge you have, the more you will do.

1001. The single and most important tip we can give you on ceramics is to have fun! When you start to make work out of it you will probably quit and that's not fun at all!

I Learned The Hard Way!

Use this handy page to make notes on things you learn by doing ceramics yourself, from teachers and from fellow ceramists.